Guide to the Best
in
Contemporary Piano Music

An Annotated List of Graded Solo Piano Music
Published Since 1950

Volume I: Levels 1 through 5

by
STANLEY BUTLER

The Scarecrow Press, Inc.
Metuchen, N. J.   1973

Library of Congress Cataloging in Publication Data

Butler, Stanley, 1914-
    Guide to the best in contemporary piano music.

    CONTENTS: v. 1. Levels 1 through 5.
    1. Piano music--Bibliography--Graded lists.
I. Title.
ML132.P3B88   016.7864'05'2   73-5693
ISBN 0-8108-0628-2

FOR CELIA

Who First Had the Idea

TABLE OF CONTENTS

PREFACE

Most of the piano students whom I first hear as entering college freshmen have little experience with contemporary music. Yet when I have carefully chosen such a work for a student, the response invariably has been enthusiastic. I am convinced that students may be more ready for contemporary music than their teachers. Many of us certainly need suggestions as to what available literature will suit our particular needs.

To further test my assumption, I conducted a day's workshop at my own university with music from American publishers. I was amazed at the number who came. Later I led sessions at two music teachers' conventions on the same subject. The response, including a number of requests for additional lists of contemporary piano music which I had distributed at the conventions, convinced me that teachers and performers were ready and eager for a selection of the better works from the mass of music published.

Fortunately I had a sabbatical leave the next year from Willamette University. I headed for Europe with letters to European publishers. The response to requests for complimentary music made mail deliveries very exciting. The response also, unfortunately, kept my wife busy wrapping and returning music of little value. Little by little I culled music from the mail deliveries and from visits to dealers, publishers, and libraries. After two months in Paris and three months in London the accumulation of music partially examined made 20 bulky packages to mail home. And to that was added more music, obtained through personal contact with publishers in New York. Obviously I had my work cut out for me for the next several years, examining and analyzing the music at my piano. How joyous have been the discoveries of fine new music!

I hope that GUIDE TO THE BEST IN CONTEMPORARY PIANO MUSIC (Volumes I and II) will suggest music which

will be considered, loved, and finally assimilated naturally
into piano teaching and performance. Easy access to music
of approximately 125 publishers from 22 countries may present challenges to your music stores. If your store can't
supply you, Joseph Boonin, Inc. and de Keyser Music will
keep the music in stock. (See page 191 for ordering in-
structions.)

There are several bases upon which the music has
been selected. Foremost, it must have revealed its expressiveness to me; it must be music which I myself would be
glad to perform or give a student. It must be in the main
stream of the diversely contemporary. Some of the works
described are conservatively contemporary, and so labelled.
I want to lure the uninitiated performer into an acquaintance
with contemporary music. I have considered works for
prepared piano outside the spectrum. There are a few
pieces with elements of improvisation or indeterminancy and
a few with a method of performance or notation different
from the traditional.

The works chosen for this Volume I range in difficulty
from those for near-beginners in level (or grade) 1 through
level 5. Grading is indeed hazardous. I have tried to be
consistent. Some idea of the difficulty of each level is suggested by comparison with the following well-known titles:

Level 1:   Kabalevsky SONG, from TWENTY-FOUR LITTLE
             PIECES, Op. 39
Level 2:   Bartók SORROW or SONG OF THE TRAMP, from
             FOR CHILDREN, vol. 2.
Level 3:   Bartók TEASING SONG, from FOR CHILDREN,
             vol. 2
Level 4:   Rebikov CHILDREN SKATING, from SILHOUETTES,
             Op. 31
Level 5:   Satie GYMNOPEDIE IN C
(Level 6:   Shostakovich FANTASTIC DANCE, Op. 1, No. 1)
(Level 7:   Ravel PAVANE POUR UNE INFANTE DEFUNTE)
(Level 8:   Griffes THE WHITE PEACOCK, from FOUR
             ROMAN SKETCHES, Op. 7).

I am most grateful to the publishers who have given
me complimentary music. Without their cooperation this
GUIDE would have been impossible. While I hoped to review
all works published from 1950 through 1968 which suit my
bases, this has obviously been impossible. There must be
omissions in my own research or incomplete exposure of pub-
lications by some publishers. I apologize to those composers

whose published works I didn't see.   However, I have been astonished to discover approximately 825 titles (479 in levels 1 through 5), among about 3000 examined, worthy of performance.   How heartening that composers will work for love, knowing there will be sketchy monetary return!   And it is encouraging, indeed, that the gambling spirit is still alive in publishers.

Regrettably, users of this GUIDE may be thwarted occasionally from purchasing a title because it is out of print temporarily or permanently.   Every effort has been made to insure each work's availability up to June, 1972. Since prices vary, none have been included.

In addition to publishers' personnel, help has come from many sources.   Election as an Atkinson Fellow at Willamette University gave me the opportunity to pursue problems in analysis.   A grant from the Shell Oil Assists Fund, administered by Willamette University's Dr. Harry Manley, helped defray expenses.   Practical assistance came from Wills Music Store, Wiltsey-Weathers Music and Berkeley Music House.

My friend Dorothy Butler edited the entire manuscript. Charles Bestor, former dean of the College of Music at Willamette University, not only assisted with some analyses but also gave generous counsel in practical matters, as did Mr. Ralph Wright, assistant to the president for university relations.   Professors Gerald Kechley and Ellis Kohs helped me clarify many a problem.   John Wiser at Joseph Boonin's gave experienced advice.   Help also came from Acting Dean Richard Stewart and Professors Raul Casillas, Paula Drayton, Clarence Kraft, Otto Mandl, Bruce McIntosh, Marion Morange, William Newman, Joseph Schnelker, Robert Stoltze, Monte Tubbs, Marija Udris, Julio Viamonte, Mr. Ladislav Bazdek, and Mr. Bennet Ludden.

It is a mystery to me how typist, teacher, and student Audrey Hultgren was able to decipher my manuscript.

Finally, my wife Celia not only endured my preoccupation but actively participated in many ways.

Stanley Butler
Willamette University
November, 1972

HOW TO USE THIS GUIDE

This GUIDE begins with the easiest compositions, Level 1, and continues through successive grades of difficulty (Volume II contains Levels 6 through 8). For easy reference, the entry number for each listing is the grade level of the piece followed by a number representing the order within that level. Thus, the first piece in the division of Level 1 is 1.1. Compositions are generally listed alphabetically by composers in each grade level. Main entry titles are given in the original language when the editor provides no English title.

Collections of works by different composers are listed at the beginning of their prevailing level. Each accepted work in such collections is reviewed under the composer's name, indicated by a direction such as "see 4.156." When the entry is a collection by a single composer, the general tenor of the collection is appraised, but to save space, only about half the works are specifically described.

Other information included:

Year composition was written, if known.
Translation of titles from the original language to English; usually also translation of performance directions.
Abbreviation for specific publisher and the number for the work in the publisher's listing, if available, is placed in parentheses immediately following review of the work. (Full names of publishers and United States agent, when appropriate, are found in the publisher information section, page 192). Date of publication and number of music pages follows publisher's name.
Number of pieces in collections.
Performance time, if indicated.
Fngr (fingering included).
MM (metronome marks included).

Ped (pedal directions included).

Anal (analysis printed with music, asterisk denotes a particularly helpful one).

Biog (biography included).

Ch (music suitable only for children).

Numbers in parentheses preceding publisher information indicate the piece on that page is not recommended. See for example the "(P 8.)" in entry 3.8.

Final numbers at end of description of a collection signify the difficulty levels of entire collection when more than one grade is included.

A title-plus-composer and composer-plus-title index is found on page 166.

Technical words (such as "coupled writing") are explained in the glossary (page 152), unless they are defined in The Harvard Brief Dictionary of Music by Willi Apel and Ralph P. Daniel, published by Harvard University Press in hard cover and Amsco Music Company and Washington Square Press in soft cover. When foreign terms are not translated, Musician's Handbook of Foreign Terms, by Christine Ammer, published in soft cover by G. Schirmer (1971), will be helpful.

Note: citations are occasionally made to works that are to be included in Volume II of this work (e.g., "8.1" or "6.6"): full data for the six collections are given beginning on page 149.

ABBREVIATIONS

acc	accompaniment
Anal	analysis
Biog	biography
Ch	for children
E	E major
e	e minor
ed	editor, edited by
Fngr	fingering
LH	left hand
MM	metronome
Ped	pedal
p	page
pp	pages
RH	right hand

1.1 BECK, MARTHA. In Old Japan.
Captures the mood of "grave dignity" and "a tinge of
sadness." In two complementing voices, both hands
are centered on same five-finger position an octave
apart. In e aeolian mode. Momentary clashes of
sevenths and ninths. Finger legato on repeated tones.
(In 2.3, 1 p.) Fngr. Biog.

1.2 FITCH, JOHN R. Five Plus Five.
Tuneful. Ingenious within clear limitations. Five
Plus Five means the ten consecutive pitches used,
LH first five of E, RH last five of G. Phrases are
usually eight measures long, with intriguingly irregular
alternation between hands and vague melody/acc identi-
fication. (Pr, 1966, 2 pp.) Fngr.

1.3 MURRAY, MILA. The Old Beggars.
Tasteful use of first five tones in d. Equal hand
emphasis. One hand holds while other moves. In
3/4, changing to 4/4 and 5/4. Whole, dotted half,
half, and quarter notes only. (LR, 1967, 2 pp.) Ch.

1.4 SALUTRINSKAYA, T. The Shepherd Plays.
An Andante cantabile dorian melody on d. LH has one
drone open fifth. Sonority emphasized by transposing
part of melody down an octave, pedal filling out ending.
Melody covers range of a tenth. (In 2.2, 1/2 p.)
Fngr, Ped.

1.5 SZELÉNYI, ISTVÁN. Musical Picture Book.
Folklike tunes, mostly in interesting scale organiza-
tions other than major and minor, have a delightful
native authenticity. Consistently tasteful settings do
justice to purity of melodies, mostly in treble.
Meters like 6/4 and 2/2, as well as short-long
rhythms. Difficulties increase gradually. This volume includes parts of two others reviewed. (See first

13

five pieces described in 2.48, first four in 3.104, and
last two in 4.152.)   Nine solos plus three pieces for
two and three performers at same piano included.
This collection, clearly printed, retains folklike music
and eliminates the most experimental.   Programmatic
titles in English and German.   Mournful Prelude is in
a five-finger position (minus second finger) on e.
Melody alternates between hands and later is in canon.
LH broken fifths ring out boldly in Ding-Dong Bells,
alternating with melody.   Each hand shifts by step
down tones of e phrygian mode.   Two augmented seconds of double harmonic scale give characteristic
flavor to Oriental Tale.   In 2/2.   For White and Black
Keys I, two two-measure fragments ingeniously complete and imitate each other.   RH in d, LH in d-sharp.
Dynamics varied.   (ScS 5770, 1967, 29 pp.)   30
pieces.   Fngr.   1, 2, 3 & 4.

1.6   WAXMAN, DONALD.   Lyric.
A forlorn Adagio.   Five-finger treble melody sensitively harmonized by descending tones of e dorian
mode.   Bass has single tones, then two and three-
tone legato chords.   Conservative.   (In 2.3, 1 p.)
Fngr.   Biog.

LEVEL 2

2.1 CLARK, FRANCES, compiler. <u>Contemporary Piano Literature,</u> Book I.
Value of this series of six books has been shown by popular use. In all books Frances Clark selected and correlated the works, Louise Goss edited and Adele deLeeuw usually wrote the biographies. Biographies and most music appealing to children. Picture of each composer included. Four of the eleven works first published after 1950 are reviewed, (see 2.29, 2.31, 2.32, 2.50)--others are too conservative. Contains music by Bartók, Kabalevsky, Kraehenbuehl, Tansman, and Tcherepnin. (SB, 1955, rev. 1961, 26 pp.) 19 pieces, 5 composers. Fngr. *Biog.

2.2. <u>Contemporary Collection,</u> No. I.
Six of twenty-six solos reviewed. (See 1.4, 2.14, 2.30, 2.33.) Other worthy numbers are too conservative or were published before 1950. Selected and edited by five individuals from prominent educational institutions. Four duet arrangements of folk tunes included. Contains music by Auguillard, Bartok, Bilohrud, Charkovsky, Erhart, Fletcher, Kabalevsky, Koch, Kraehenbuehl, Lukewitz, Moffatt, Owen, Salutrinskaya, Sternklar, Wehr, and Ziller. (SB, 1963, 31 pp.) 30 pieces, 16 composers. Fngr, some Ped. 2, some 1.

2.3 <u>New Scribner Music Library,</u> Vol. I, For Beginners, ed. by Merle Montgomery.
Very practical collection. Twenty-seven works by seventeen composers contemporary enough for review. (See 1.1, 1.6, 2.4, 2.6, 2.7, 2.8, 2.16, 2.18, 2.19, 2.21, 2.22, 2.23, 2.34, 2.42, 2.51, 2.52, 2.53, 2.54, 2.55, 3.24, 3.54, 3.111, 3.113.) Editor's preface states: "... one hundred and eighty-six [works] are new and published for the first time. Virtually all of the new pieces were written especially for this volume

15

by forty gifted American composers." Many practical
pedagogical needs admirably filled. Biographies of the
forty American composers included. Contains works by
Ahrendt, Alt, Appledorn, Bach, Bacon, Beck, Beck-
helm, Beethoven, Bernardone, Bezdek, Campbell, Clark,
Clementi, Crist, Derleth, Dvorkin, Ezell, Frackenpohl,
George, Gillock, Gurlitt, Handel, Hanson, Haydn, How-
ard, Kilpatrick, Kramer, Kullak, La Montaine, Lincoln,
MacKown, McKay, McKinney, Mills, Phillips, Procter
A, Procter L, Reinecke, Rice, Scharwenka, Schumann,
Sifler, Smith, Spilman, Spindler, Thomé, Van Slyck,
Von Weber, Washburn, Watson, Waxman, Werder, and
Winogron. (This volume is purchasable only in a sub-
scription series of ten volumes. [Possible minor inac-
curacies in description due to revision in progress.])
(Scribner's, 1964, 238 pp.) 207 works, 54 composers.
Fngr, some MM & Ped. Biog. Many Ch. 2, some 1,
3 & 4.

2.4   ALT, HANSI.   Sleepyhead.
Lovely work.   Phrygian character established by second measure.   Treble melody often top tone of two- or
three-tone chord.   Single note acc often on offbeat.
Middle section accompanied by slow trill on lowered
tonic tone, piece's only accidental.   (In 2.3, 1 p.)
Fngr.   Biog.

2.5   BACON, ERNST.   Melodious Sonnett.
This graceful music teaches much.   Melody is heard
first with no acc, then repeated in three settings: (a)
as thumb tones alternating between hands in eighth note
rhythm, (b) in broken chord triplets, and (c) in contrasting material using legato and staccato at same time.
In e aeolian mode, but ending on minor dominant. (Pr,
1963, 2 pp.)   MM.

2.6   BACON, ERNST.   The White Church.
Dignity and some originality are attained by simplest
means in this conservative work.   Excellent for hand
independence in two-voice texture.   In F with a few accidentals.   (In 2.3, 1 p.)   Fngr.   Biog.

2.7   CAMPBELL, ALINE.   A Camel Ride.
Ostinato bass with long-short rhythm creates descriptive motion "humpily," as directions state.   Augmented
seconds associated with the near-East depict the camel.
Surprise skips in melody.   In two voices.   Conserva-

tive. (In 2.3, 1 p.) Fngr. Biog. Ch.

2.8 CLARK, ELIZABETH. The Rocking Chair.
Smooth, uneventful motion, as the title suggests. In
pure dorian, five-finger position only, LH on a, RH on
c. Hands sometimes in coupled tenths. Some short-
long rhythm. Soft pedal used. (In 2.3, 1 p.) Fngr.
Biog.

2.9 DIEMER, EMMA LOU. Gigue.
Brilliant and spontaneous. "4-note chord clusters in
each hand, and accents on first of group of 3 eighth
notes" require finger strength. No thumb under. Mirror, imitation, and coupled techniques. In lydian and
mixolydian mode. (B&H, 1962, 2 pp.) Fngr. Anal.

2.10 DIEMER, EMMA LOU. Invention.
Sensitively expressive and technically useful. Middle
section has lovely color chords. "Technical features
emphasized: 5-note scale figures in both hands, 2-
note slow trills in both hands." Two voices, 2/2
meter. In d dorian mode. (B&H, 1962, 2 pp.) Fngr.
Anal.

2.11 DIEMER, EMMA LOU. Serenade.
Splendid craftsmanship in this graceful number. Original use of familiar materials. Uses legato seventh
reach. Seventh chords arranged in slurred thirds.
Equal hand emphasis. "Technical features emphasized:
singing melody in one hand--accompanying figure in
other hand, irregular meter." (B&H, 1962, 2 pp.)
Fngr. Anal.

2.12 EL-DABH, HALIM. Mekta' in the Art of Kita, Books
I and II.
Title might be translated as "The Microcosm in the
Art of Macrocosm." Intention is to present Egyptian
ideas (composer is Egyptian) in Western music; interest will be in the exotic music, rather than its pianistic appeal. Two lines appear in a severe union in first
book. Tone clusters appear in second book. (Pet
6184, 1961, 4 pp.) 6 pieces. MM. Anal, *Biog.
2 & 3.

2.13 FINE, IRVING. Lullaby for a Baby Panda.
"Delicately tinted" music. Lyrical treble melody.
Only single notes or fifths in LH; straying from five-

finger position is by step.   RH slight exploration beyond five-finger position.   Simplest of rhythms.   Conservative.   (Pr. 1958--also in 3.1, 2 pp.)   Fngr,
MM.   *Anal.   Ch.

2.14 FLETCHER, STANLEY. Dusk.
Moderate originality in this thoughtful work.   Only at
end is aeolian mode (picardy third, however) revealed.
"Dolce espressivo" bass melody has no repetitions or
cadences.   RH repeats two legato thirds.   Direction of
"con pedale" is puzzling.   (In 2.2, 1 p.) Fngr.

2.15 FRACKENPOHL, ARTHUR. Circus Parade.
Good taste shown in these appealing pieces.   Slightly exploratory harmony only element not conservative.   Triads often move in parallel motion by seconds.   Modal
influences.   Melody hand has no acc.   Pedal usually not
necessary.   Splendid illustrative drawings.   Left Foot
First uses forearm staccatos, particularly with LH
fifths.   In C, with striking digressions.   LH melody and
RH staccato triads found in Air for South Paw.   In lydian mode.   Follow the Leader is a "moderately slow,"
naturally flowing canon for two voices in dorian mode.
Oriental Two-Step is in pentatonic mode in black keys.
LH forearm staccato with an ostinato pattern of fifths.
Every Step a Whole Step has ostinato pattern and invertible counterpoint.   Dress to the Right is vigorous with
RH triads and much bass motion by fourths.   In G mixolydian mode.   Has the only octaves in collection.   (Oxf,
1960, 14 pp.)   13 pieces.   Fngr.   Ch. 2 & 3.

2.16 FRACKENPOHL, ARTHUR. Large Seconds and Polka.
If thumbs are centered on A (octave apart here), and
fingers spread out by Large Seconds, whole tone scale
will result.   In two voices, with octaves, augmented
fifths and major thirds for harmonic intervals.   "Flowing" motion from triple meter, and,quarter, half and
dotted-half notes.   Polka is tuneful and "lively."   Traditional, except for lydian mode in section A.   A is
noticeable also for syncopations.   RH has melody in section A, LH in B.   Mostly in five-finger position (In
2.3, 1 p. & 1 p.) Fngr. Biog.

2.17 FRACKENPOHL, ARTHUR. Sharp Four.
"Moderately fast," sprightly music.   Title refers to
characteristic raised fourth of lydian mode.   Melody in
five-finger position.   Equal hand emphasis.   Simplest

alternation between legato and staccato. (LR, 1965,
2 pp.) Fngr. Ch.

2.18 GEORGE, EARL. Waltzing with Father.
In this amusing number father waltzes, but not gracefully. Accompanying thirds on second and third beats
not in harmony with melody; instead, they plod up and
down in alternate hands. C melody has five-finger as-
cents and descents. (In 2.3, 1 p.) Fngr, MM. Ch.
Biog.

2.19 GILLOCK, WILLIAM L. The Prowling Pussy Cat.
Title "stealthily" portrayed. Sforzando raised fourth
helps characterization in section A. Whole tone scales
ascend hand over hand in section B, with pedal de-
pressed. Range moderately wide. Touch and dynamics
varied. (In 2.3, 1 p.) Fngr, Ped. Ch. Biog.

2.20 GOULD, MORTON. At the Piano, Book 2.
Youthful and appealing. Explores dissonance, partly
caused by conflicts where ostinatos are much used.
Rhythms traditional, except for one meter in 5/8 and
another alternating between 4/8 and 5/8. Melody usually in treble. Waltz is good example of dissonance
exploration. When melody of third phrase ends, acc,
moving by parallel triads, is first consonant, then dissonant. Only white keys used. A Rough Game, marked
"fast and brisk," is an interesting study in contrary and
parallel motion. In two-part texture. Resembles super locrian scale. In the "gracefully moving" Rocking
in 5/8 meter, groupings shift from three plus two to
two plus three. Contrary motion and coupled writing
prominent. Suave and "fast moving" A Special Special
has much chromatic motion. Slurring changes when
phrases are repeated. (G&C, 1964, 15 pp.) 9 pieces.
Fngr, some Ped. 2, 3 & 4.

2.21 HANSON, HOWARD. The Big Bell and the Little
Bells.
Superior imagination. One chord with added second and
sixth sounds The Big Bell, which alternates, pedal
held, with higher broken fifths sounding The Little Bell.
Practice for shift between low and medium registers,
and also for alternating hands. (In 2.3, 1 p.) Fngr,
Ped. Anal. Biog. Ch.

2.22 HANSON, HOWARD. Horn Calls in the Forest.

Bright peals of melodic tritones in dotted rhythm depict
title. Strength needed for accented tones. At times
RH is softened to an echo. (In 2.3, 1/2 p.) Fngr.
Anal. Biog. Ch.

2.23 HANSON, HOWARD. Tricks or Treats.
This economical little piece has much to teach. The
one line of music is played by alternating hands using
first three fingers only. Ascending or descending minor
seconds arranged in 7/8 measures. Fine for crescendo
and decrescendo. (In 2.3, 1/2 p.) Fngr. Anal.
Biog. Ch.

2.24 HOPKINS, ANTHONY. For Talented Beginners, Book 1.
Original and imaginative material designed for orderly
exploration of piano keyboard. Six pieces confined to
one melodic and/or harmonic interval, progressing
from Single Notes through to Sixths. Variety in dynamics. Half note used for beat in four pieces. Progres-
sively more difficult. Modernisms should be no problem. Groping described by harmonics (fifths, or fourth
chords) which, before settling in the "right" place, are
too high or low. Thirds is gentle tone study of black
key seventh and ninth chords blended by pedal. Fourths,
marked "strongly rhythmical and fairly fast," is vigorous and harsh. Four-tone chords, usually fourth apart,
are often repeated rapidly in forearm strokes. Fifths
has splendid sonority and climax, and striking variety
with broken and unbroken fifth. Spontaneous and rhythmically stirring, the bravura Getting Difficult has accented broken fifths and sixths, repeated staccato intervals, and coupled writing. (Oxf, 1963, 11 pp.) 10
pieces. Fngr, some Ped. 2 & 3.

2.25 JÁRDÁNYI, PÁL. Opening Bud and Hoppity, Hoppity,
Hop!
Opening Bud is a poetic Andante tranquillo in 2/2.
Various chromatic changes create illusory quality in
treble melody. Has augmented seconds and tritones.
Fun and lively action in second work. Single forearm
staccato tones alternate between hands, or fifths repeated in both hands. In lydian mode. (In 4.8, 2/3 p.
& 1 p.) Fngr. *Biog.

2.26 KARKOFF, MAURICE. 15 Latta Pianostycken.
15 Easy Piano Pieces, refreshingly naive, often sound
like folk songs. Tunes are modal--aeolian, mixolydian,

dorian or lydian. Traditional piano writing with various textures--melody with no acc or simple chord acc, as well as two-part imitation. Two duets. Titles in English and Swedish. The Tin Soldier's March has harmonic fifths for acc, moving up and down a fifth or fourth. Echo Answers in the Woods has dotted rhythm commonly found in 6/8 meter. Raindrops uses forearm staccatos on repeated tones. Single tone acc on offbeats. In the jolly Playing Tig, RH often uses hand staccato, LH always legato. LH has reach of broken major seventh. (Geh, 1961, 14 pp.) Ch.

2.27 KARKOFF, MAURICE. Little Kaleidoscope (1956-57). Poetic, imaginative and original with exotic chromatic explorations. In foreword (in Swedish), composer tells of his free tonal, modal, Oriental, and twelve-tone writing. Aside from a few meter changes, rhythms are traditional. Titles in English and Swedish. Grey Clouds offers opportunity for arm weight pivoting between white and black keys. Expressive melody alternates between hands. In The Solitary Island pedal blends consecutive tones of scale in varied note lengths. Scale has two augmented seconds. In the poetic The Oasis, repeated tones held by pedal are used as a segment in twelve-tone set. Modal Merry Dance is sturdy with acc of parallel fifths. Syncopated melody. Charles's Wain (otherwise known as The Big Dipper), has arpeggiated ninth and eleventh chords changing for color; tonality obscure. Also polychords. The Maestoso, marchlike In Front of the Castle sounds Oriental. Two-measure melodic fragment heard in coupled fifths and fourths, as well as in three parts with prominent contrary motion. The Goblin Dance is droll with oom-pah-pah or oom-pah acc. Chromaticisms, augmented seconds, patterns covering a tritone, and sudden shorter note values aid in depicting title. (Geh, 1967, 18 pp.) 18 pieces. Fngr, MM, some Ped. 2, 3 & 4.

2.28 KONOWITZ, BERT. Blue Note Boogie. Has fine relaxed swing. Many dotted notes in each hand. Could be used to correct a RH low fifth finger knuckle, since that finger is usually on a black key. (LR, 1964, 2 pp.) Fngr.

2.29 KRAEHENBUEHL, DAVID. Bulldozer (1960). This fine boy's music in G slides down to F-sharp for contrast. RH broken chord melody, with LH acc using

harmonic fifths and sixths two octaves lower. In 5/4
meter, with beats grouped by two plus three, or three
plus two--otherwise music is conservative. (In 2.1,
1 p.) Fngr. *Biog. Ch.

2.30 KRAEHENBUEHL, DAVID. Scherzo on Tenth Avenue,
      Dream World and Snowfall.
      Lively rhythms in Scherzo on Tenth Avenue played
      "with a steady bounce." Rests of several beats follow
      fastest tones; rests also on first beats. Coupled writ-
      ing in tenths. Hands have two different five-finger posi-
      tions. Forearm non-legato strokes. Dream World
      mood is consistently illusionary. Many parallel sev-
      enths, arranged as fifths in each hand. Fine pedal
      study. Melody uses fifth and fourth fingers for upper
      tones of harmonic fifths. Snowfall conveys delicate
      mood by long pedal blends of unrelated broken triads
      alternating between hands. Played "slowly and gently,"
      useful for controlling pp. (In 2.2, 1 p, 1 p & 1 p.)
      Fngr, some Ped.

2.31 KRAEHENBUEHL, DAVID. Sleeping Beauty (1960).
      Provides excellent black key practice. In aeolian mode
      on d-sharp, with pedal tone on third of tonic. Lowered
      leading tone over tonic harmonies. RH has uncompli-
      cated broken chord melody and LH simplest double
      notes, with one tone held while second moves. (In 2.1,
      1 p.) Fngr. *Biog.

2.32 KRAEHENBUEHL, DAVID. Whistlin' Tune (1960).
      Irresistible tune, marked "gaily." Melody divided be-
      tween hands with no acc. In d aeolian mode with color
      contrast. Simplest 6/8 meter. (In 2.1, 1 p.) Fngr.
      *Biog. Ch.

2.33 LUKEWITZ, JOSEPH. Three Pieces.
      First Piece in pure d dorian mode. Upper of two
      voices has some rhythmic independence. Third Piece,
      a lovely Lento, is in pure e phrygian mode. Rhythms
      have tones tied across bar-line, or through main beats.
      (In 2.2, 2 pp.) Fngr.

2.34 McKAY, GEORGE FREDERICK. Morning Hymn.
      Superior melodic sense. In pure e phrygian mode.
      Melody usually in RH without acc, although cadences
      have three-tone chords. (In 2.3, 1 p.) Fngr. Biog.

2.35 McKAY, GEORGE FREDERICK. Prairie Vista.
Moderato pastorale. Fine tone study for melody alone
in RH. LH acc often three-tone chords of gentle coloring. Settles at end on a, but whether mode is primarily phrygian on a, mixolydian on C, or otherwise else-
where is interestingly uncertain. (Pr, 1964--also in
3.61, 2 pp.) Some Fngr.

2.36 MARIENNE, SISTER. Fanfare, Sick on Saturday and
       Juggling.
Accessible, fine introduction to twelve-tone music.
Three different sets used; segments of each set are
found, including hexachords in Sick on Saturday. Mirror principle used in all pieces. Virtually only five
finger position. Forearm staccato and finger legato on
repeated tones. (LR, 1967, 3 pp.) Fngr. *Anal. Ch.

2.37 MARIENNE, SISTER. Hurry Up!, Moon Dreaming,
       and Motorcycles.
Spontaneously depicting titles, "this set of pieces illus-
trate a tone row ... and the retrograde of a tone
row...." Motorcycles further illustrates how order of
tones may be changed. Not much pedal. Hurry Up!
has LH trill with first and second fingers. Motorcycles
has rapid alternations between hands. (LR, 1967, 3
pp.) Fngr, Ped. *Anal. Ch.

2.38 MILLS, JOAN GEILFUSS. Phrygian Fable.
Expressive melody in g phrygian mode. Skillful shifts
to tonality. Melody has many repeated tones, LH acc
only open fifths. Meter changes between 5/8 and 2/8.
(LR, 1964, 2 pp.) Ch.

2.39 PHILLIPS, BURRILL. Little Song.
Classic serenity, with variety. In two voices, LH acc
like an Alberti bass. In G--no accidentals. Conservative. (EV, 1955, 2 pp.)

2.40 RICCARDI, JOSEPH. Playful Kitten.
This work, centered on F, wavers cleverly between
phrygian and major modes. Legato melody tones alternate with hand staccato thirds. Equal hand emphasis.
Rhythm traditional. (EV, 1964, 2 pp.) Ch.

2.41 RICCARDI, JOSEPH. Recess Time.
Swings happily from hand to hand, RH leading. Very
consistent. Allegro has telling play with cross rela-

tions.   In F.   Phrases frequently cover only a third or
fourth, with easy lateral shifts of a second, third or
fourth between phrases.   Rhythms almost exclusively
two eighths and a quarter in each hand, hands overlapping.   (Pr, 1964, 2 pp.)   MM, Ped.   Ch.

2.42 RICE, THOMAS N.   Choral Anthem and Two-Keys
        Etude.
      Choral Anthem has free association of familiar triads,
      although melody restricted to upper four tones of aeol-
      ian mode.   Offers legato practice with three and four-
      tone chords and pedal practice.   Half and whole notes
      only.   All stops are out in the slashing ff Two-Keys
      Etude, played "as fast as you can."   While LH jabs
      out the sforzando melody in C-sharp, RH uses staccato
      broken fifths on D tonic chord in same range.   (In 2.3,
      1 p. & 1 p.)   Fngr, some Ped.

2.43 RICKER, EARL.   Ghosts on the Stairs.
      RH staccato broken chord melody creates weird sounds
      of activated overtones, while I, IV 6/4 or V 6/5 chords
      are silently depressed.   (LR, 1966, 2 pp.)   Fngr, MM.
      Ch.

2.44 RICKER, EARL.   The Lonesome Prairie.
      Captures mood of loneliness.   Melody based on D and f-
      sharp triads.   LH harmonic fifths, moving unconcerned-
      ly by step or half step, illustrate unconstrained ways of
      harmonizing melody (polyharmony).   (LR, 1967, 2 pp.)
      Fngr, MM.   Ch.

2.45 STARER, ROBERT.   Syncopated Serenade.
      Treble melody has jazz syncopation, and frequent flatted
      inflections of third, fifth (here sharped fourth) and sev-
      enth of blues scale.   Bass keeps beat with harmonic
      triads moving by step.   In C.   (LR, 1964, 2 pp.)

2.46 STEVENS, HALSEY.   Five Little Five-Finger Pieces
        (1954).
      Lyrical music both original and rooted in tradition.   In
      II, RH uses first five tones of D, and LH third through
      seventh tones.   I is a mirror canon, III and IV have
      imitation.   I is in b, III appears to be in lochrian mode,
      IV is lydian and V major.   2/2 and 5/4 meter signa-
      tures.   Total is fine teaching material for developing
      legato, equal hand skill and unusual five-finger positions.
      (Hel, 1960, 5 pp.)   2 min.   Fngr, MM.

2.47 SUGÁR, REZSÖ. <u>Imitation I and Imitation II.</u>
The inventive Andante <u>Imitation I</u> uses imitation between
two voices in every other phrase.   Hands alternate in
leading unusual small-step explorations among black
keys.   <u>Imitation II</u> is a marcato Allegro moderato in
two voices.   Twelve-measure melody is in scale related to Hungarian Major, except seventh degree is
raised.   Melody in coupled writing, then in imitation
at the octave, tenth, and last by inversion at the octave.   Rapid five-finger work.   (In 4.8, 1/2 p. & 2
pp.)   Fngr.   2 & 5.

2.48 SZELÉNYI, ISTVÁN.   <u>Forty Short Piano Pieces for</u>
      <u>Beginners,</u> Book I.
(See 1.5 for general remarks.)   No key signatures
used, although only one piece uses more than one sharp
or one flat.   More music appears on page than usual.
Titles in English, Hungarian and German.   Poignant
<u>Love Ditty</u> is in d Hungarian minor with clear four-
measure phrases.   Melody airily tossed between hands
in <u>Merry-Go-Round</u>.   In mode resembling phrygian, but
with raised sixth.   <u>Pipe Sounds</u> "from far away" has
beautiful melody with short-long rhythms.   Purity
comes from tones of aeolian mode (one exception) and
from acc of fifths.   <u>The Anvil Clangs</u> pounds with un-
ending vigor.   In pure a aeolian mode, it develops
strength and rotary motion.   <u>In the Train</u> uses perpetual motion and coupled writing to sound the locomotive
clatter.   Played Allegro di molto.   Useful for strength-
ening weaker fingers and for contractions.   (Above
pieces also in 1.5.)   "Scherzando" <u>With Two Balls</u> is
a tricky canon.   When in major mode, alternation between lowered third and raised fourth steps is delightful.   <u>All the Twelve Tones</u> in key of C provides free-
ing experience using all twelve tones.   Excellent for
two-part playing with contrary motion and a canon.
(EMB, 1957, 15 pp.)   20 pieces.   Fngr.   2 & 3, some
4.

2.49 TAJČEVIĆ, MARKO.   <u>First Suite.</u>
Likeable folk-sounding tunes with suitable ostinato acc.
White keys only, five-finger positions predominate.
Tunes always in treble.   Con moto first movement in
dorian mode.   LH slow trill acc.   Andantino is in
phrygian mode, with LH ostinato acc exercising fourth
and fifth fingers.   <u>Allegro</u> is in mixolydian mode.   One
acc pattern is four-tone ostinato, going its way despite

frequent meter changes in tune. (In 4.12, 3 pp.) 3
movements. Fngr. Biog. Ch. 2 & 3.

2.50 TCHEREPNIN, ALEXANDER. Joy and Tears (1954).
Music expresses Joy by repeated seventh and ninth
chords, with loud forearm staccato touch. Tears has
soft double notes in each hand, moving legato and in
contrary motion. In e aeolian mode--no accidentals.
(In 2.1, 1 p.) Fngr. *Biog.

2.51 WASHBURN, ROBERT. Up and Down.
Allegro is moderately contemporary, yet uses only
tones of G. Different five-finger patterns ingeniously
pursued. Mostly quarter note contrary motion between
hands, with alternate activity. Both staccato and legato, loud and soft. Conservative. (Oxf, 1964--also
in 2.3, 1 p.) Fngr. Biog.

2.52 WATSON, SCOTT. Ballad.
Lovely treble melody usually uses different five-finger
patterns. In pure d dorian mode. LH detached double
note acc. (In 2.3, 1 p.) Fngr. Biog.

2.53 WATSON, SCOTT. Parade Time.
"Strict march time, without expression" is the indication of great seriousness for this little number. Ostinato LH acc includes harmonic minor second. Melody
has fourths. In C (no accidentals) although melody
ends on F. (In 2.3, 1 p.) Fngr. Biog. Ch.

2.54 WAXMAN, DONALD. Sad Daydream.
Gentle polyharmonies, such as simultaneous tonic and
dominant harmonies on last chord, bring expressiveness. Unpredictable chromaticisms. Pianistic explorations include legato three, four and five-tone chords.
(In 2.3, 1 p.) Fngr. Biog.

2.55 WAXMAN, DONALD. Three Conversations: Friendly,
      Angry, Jolly.
Excellent spontaneous study for finger facility with rotary motion, rapid two-note slurs, and alternating
hands. Tonal. Conservative. (In 2.3, 2 pp.) Fngr.
Biog. Ch.

3.1 American Music by Distinguished Composers, Book 1,
   ed by Isadore Freed.
   Splendid cross-section of works by serious composers
   at a low price. Five works reviewed. (See 2.13,
   3.30, 3.31, 3.60, 4.65.) Contains music by Cowell,
   Fine, Fletcher, Freed, Haufrecht, Luening, and Mc-
   Kay. (Pr, 1964, 15 pp.) 8 pieces, 7 composers.
   Fngr, some MM & Ped. *Anal. 3, some 2 & 4.

3.2 Canadian Festival Album, Vol. 1.
   Three numbers reviewed. (See 3.44, 4.44, and 4.74.)
   Others too conservative. Contains music by Bayley,
   Coulthard, De Coursey, Dolin, Fiala, Harmer, Jaque,
   Joachim, and Slater. (BMI, 1964, 19 pp.) 10 pieces,
   9 composers. Fngr, some MM and Ped. 3, some 4.

3.3 CLARK, FRANCES, compiler. Contemporary Piano
   Literature, Book 2.
   (See 2.1.) Louise Goss replaces Adele deLeeuw.
   Two of the five works first published after 1950 are
   reviewed. (See 3.106 and 3.108.) Others too con-
   servative. Contains music by Bartók, Kabalevsky,
   Shostakovich, Siegmeister, Tansman, and Tcherepnin.
   (SB, 1955, 24 pp.) 17 pieces, 6 composers. Fngr.
   *Biog.

3.4 CLARK, FRANCES, compiler. Contemporary Piano
   Literature, Book 3.
   (See 2.1.) Three of five works first published after
   1950 are reviewed. (See 3.64 and 3.109.) Others too
   conservative. Contains music by Bartók, Gretchaninov,
   Kabalevsky, Moore, Scott, Shostakovich, and Tcherep-
   nin. (SB, 1957, 36 pp.) 23 pieces, 7 composers.
   Fngr, Ped. *Biog.

3.5 CLARK, FRANCES, compiler. Contemporary Piano

27

Literature, Book 4.
(See 2.1.) All nine works first published after 1950
reviewed. (See 3.28, 3.65, and 4.156.) Contains
music by Bartók, Finney, Gretchaninov, Kabalevsky,
Moore, Prokofiev, Stravinsky, and Tcherepnin. (SB,
1957, 43 pp.) 27 pieces, 8 composers. Fngr, Ped.
*Biog. 3 & 4.

3.6 DESCAVES, LUCETTE, ed. Les Contemporains,
      Premier Recueil.
      The Contemporaries, first collection, highly recom-
      mended for French taste at this level of difficulty.
      Twelve works reviewed. (See 3.17, 3.20, 3.55, 3.62,
      4.53, 4.77, 4.99, 5.37, 5.77, 5.80, 5.104, and 5.112.)
      Pieces not reviewed are skillful, but too conservative.
      About half the works suitable only for children. Al-
      ways tonal and usually in homphonic texture. More
      music on each page than customary. Modernisms
      pleasantly cloaked. Graceful remarks in French about
      each composer and work by Daniel Lesur. Contains
      music by Arrieu, Beaucamp, Chailley, Damase, Des-
      champs, Garcin, Jolivet, Landowsky, Lantier, Lavagne,
      Lesur, Martinon, Maurice, Milhaud, Pascal, Poulenc,
      Sancan, Sauget, Thierac, and Thiriet. Titles in
      French, English, German, and Spanish. (Noël, 1950,
      34 pp.) 20 pieces, 20 composers. Fngr, some MM,
      Ped. 3, 4 & 5.

3.7 ARCHER, VIOLET. Four Little Studies.
      One number titled A Little Different: apt description
      for all four pieces. Much freedom, indeed, in the
      tonal harmony. Follow the Leader is first in a canon
      at the seventh; later, by inversion a sixteenth lower;
      at end the canon is broken, replaced by mysterious
      harmonies. In the Allegro Bouncing Lightly staccato
      thirds alternate between hands, often only minor sec-
      ond away from two-part coupled writing. (Wat, 1964,
      2 pp.) MM. 3, some 2.

3.8 BACON, ERNST. Friends.
      Discerning works with clear aims, proving something
      new can be done with familiar methods. Natural musi-
      cality and fine unity of materials. Organized around
      sound pedagogical values. Modal hints. Much pianis-
      tic variety, such as singing touch, equal hand empha-
      sis, and slight extensions. Foreword and brief com-
      ment for each work. Harmonies and changing keys in

Thinking are tantalizing. Friends, the title piece,
graceful and "breezily" moving, contrasts simultaneous
"staccato against legato." Hands exchange roles.
Follow the Leader does just that, in two-part imitation. So many keys visited that amusing satiety almost stops the excursions. Wonderfully "spirited"
Exhilaration (early American folk song, one of two in
collection) has appropriate bass of "extended" broken
fifths. RH broken chord melody also has extensions.
In B-flat--no accidentals. (P 8.) (FC, 1963, 8 pp.)
8 pieces. Anal. Ch. 3, some 2.

3.9   BADEN, CONRAD. 10 Småstykker for Klaver.
10 Small Pieces for Piano will appeal to children. Obviously tonal, with ear-catching chromaticism; modal
also. Rhythms and style of piano writing traditional.
Titles in Norwegian. Heavy Load (2) never escapes
from the repetition of LH legato harmonic sixths and
fifths. Mood of Hotspur (or Spit Fire) (3) captured
by accented dissonant first beats and by insistent repeated tones. In g with lowered second and raised
fourth. Song of Autumn (9) has lovely melody with
harmonies searching throughout, avoiding the obvious
g, and finally stopping with C. Perpetual motion Ac-
quariam (10) alternates briskly between hands; has
brief RH rotary motion. Translations are Squirrel
(1), Darling Hare (4), Waltz (5), Melody (6), Play at
Hopscotch (7), and On the Train (8). (Norsk, 1968,
6 pp.) Ch.

3.10   BADINGS, HENK. Arcadia II.
This fine music wisely explores piano range within controlled limits; freed from major-minor domination.
Subtitle is 10 Five-Tone Pieces on 10 Keys. Both
hands have five-finger positions, sometimes same,
sometimes different, notated separately at head of each
work. Both hands have same modes (lydian, phrygian,
super locrian, and Neapolitan minor), but also have,
at times, different modes. Fast works, like Rigaudon
and Country Dance, are straightforward and high spirited, calling for finger facility. Slow works, like
Arietta and Elegy, require tone and dynamic attention.
Double note acc used. Seven works use only treble
staff. No pedal needed. (ScS 4177, 1951, 6 pp.)
10 pieces. Fngr. 3, some 2.

3.11 BADINGS, HENK. Arcadia III.
Attractive music of enduring taste. Consistent piano
technique. Splendid pedagogical planning. Folk (often
modal) and Oriental influences. Five-finger positions
shift up and down, no extensions, no thumb under.
Pedal unnecessary. Chords usually have only two
tones, and often retain a common tone. Burlesca is
rhythmically challenging in its starting and stopping
and varied articulations. Exotic Song's (also in 4.9)
mournful melody in synthetic and varied scale, is in
LH, RH having ostinato acc exercising independent
fifth finger. Notturno also exotic, with many diminished fourths and fifths in melody. Rather difficult
pp, legato acc of slow trill alternates between hands.
Brilliant Fanfare has rapidly repeated marcato chords
and fast broken triads. Clear ABA form, A in lydian
mode. Scherzo filled with vital ideas. First figure
binds whole together. Sforzandos and sudden f measures interrupt leggiero flow. (ScS 4178, 1951, 11 pp.)
10 pieces. Fngr. 3, some 2 & 5.

3.12 BENNETT, RICHARD RODNEY. Diversions.
Attractive use made of familiar techniques. Several
pieces end with modal cadences. Neo-classic. Jaunty
III "ritmico" has dotted rhythms. Harmonies wander
far from tonic key of d. IV is lyrical, its moderately exploratory finger patterns in legato double notes.
Seventh chords used. VII a youthful Vivace in 5/8.
Many harmonic seconds alternate between hands.
Coupled writing. Fine dynamic variety. (UE 14151,
1965, 7 pp.) 7 pieces, 6 min, 15 sec. Fngr, MM,
some Ped. 3 & 4.

3.13 BERGER, BERT. 10 Oefeningen.
Frère Jacques is woven into bass of two of these 10
Exercises, as fundamental as folk tunes, title notwith-
standing. Excellent introduction to modes, three specifically so. Otherwise, modal influences as well as
some chromaticisms supply slightly exotic character.
Rhythm not adventurous. Pianistic basis is five-finger
position with modest departures. Some double notes.
Hands nearly equal in almost entirely legato compositions. Conservative. (B&VP 834, 1966, 6 pp.) Fngr.

3.14 BERKOWITZ, SOL. March of the Puppets.
Extrovert and accessible. Simple rhythmic motive
sometimes tossed back and forth between hands. At

other times harmonic seconds accompany a widely-
spaced bass line.   Key is C, with polytonal implica-
tions never quite confirmed.   (In 4.1, 2 pp.)   Fngr.
Biog. Ch.

3.15 BIALOSKY, MARSHALL.   Five Western Scenes.
Irresistible boys' music, authentic, accessible, imaginative, and youthful.   Both bold and lyric.   Reminds
one of Copland.   No troublesome modernisms.   Uses
octaves.   Alone on the Prairie has poignant mood.
In traditional G, no accidentals; nevertheless, contemporary, such as ending of third phrase on mediant
seventh chord.   A Tall Tale strides up and down in
bass, with broken chord melody, audacious key shifts,
and lydian mode.   (Gal, 1965, 8 pp.)   MM.   Ch. 3 &
4.

3.16 BORGULYA, ANDRÁS.   The Frisky Bunny.
Playful, free use of all twelve tones in C-sharp.   Much
hand alternation with single notes and thirds.   Many
non-legato broken chords.   Treble range only.   (In 4.8,
1 p.)   Fngr.   Ch.

3.17 CHAILLEY, JACQUES.   Little Red Riding Hood.
Imaginative number, with performer or someone else
reciting story (given in French) while music is performed.   Mild modernisms, such as doubly infected
and altered chords, often related to story.   Parallel
legato harmonic thirds, fourths and fifths.   (In 3.6, 2
pp.)   Fngr.   Ch.

3.18 CONSTANTINIDIS, YANNIS.   Greek Miniatures, Vol.
1 (1948-51).
Beautiful melodies stressed in settings true to folk
spirit.   Tunes ingeniously depend much on fingers and
held tones for fullness.   Many ornaments used.   Often
modal, particularly aeolian.   Irregular meters like
5/8 and 7/8.   Sometimes two pieces grouped together.
Meticulous editing; exact pedaling, for instance.   Too
many pieces at one time may be monotonous, since
neither range nor key selection is wide.   Modernisms
are conservative.   In this volume most melodies in the
treble.   Usually no more than three voices, with reach
rarely beyond broken seventh.   One hand usually concerned only with melody.   Insistent rhythm in III with
characteristic short-long lengths and acc leading toward longest tones.   VI has slurred two-tone intervals.

Equal hand emphasis. VII, in pure phrygian mode on
a, flows smoothly. Allegro giocoso VIII gives practice
for RH legato thirds. Allegretto XV, played "with humour," has both legato and staccato thirds for LH acc.
XVI in 7/8 meter, grouped by three plus four. Texture filled out by parallel thirds with melody, and by
held tones. (Ron, 1957, 14 pp.) 16 pieces, 10 min.
Fngr, MM, Ped. 3, 4 & 5.

3.19 DELLO JOIO, NORMAN. Suite for the Young.
Genuinely childlike pieces in excellent taste could serve
as gentle introduction to some contemporary tonal prac-
tices. Pianistic values absolutely solid. Two-part
Invention "on a major and minor triadic melody" has
triads imitated in contrary motion. In unmetered
Echoes "do not count--let the ear determine how to
achieve the echo effect." LH leads, with echo much
higher at compound tritone. Moving parallel to melody
of A Sad Tale is a third and a fourth. Ostinato of
fourths used in LH. Spontaneous Small Fry catches
essentials of the Blues: notes of lowered third (here
raised second) and lowered sevenths, syncopation, and
ostinato bass using traditional I-IV-I-V-I progression.
Chorale Chant "has been set to the rhythm of the words
of the Lord's Prayer." Four voices in chromatic harmony move small distances in same rhythm. Seventh
chords often used. (Mrk, 1964, 10 pp.) 10 pieces.
Fngr, MM. Anal. Ch. 3 & 4.

3.20 DESCHAMPS, JACQUELINE. Dance of the Pickaninny
Stolen by the Gipsies.
Music of obvious appeal. In g aeolian mode. LH acc
uses minor second clash. Forearm non-legato. Fair-
ly wide range. Conservative. (In 3.6, 2 pp.) Fngr.
Ch.

3.21 DIEMENTE, EDWARD. Restless Motion.
Haunting and serious piece in slow tempo. Interesting
counterpoint using two recurring four-tone motives.
Tonality uncertain, perhaps deliberately, because of
major/minor conflict. Uses triplets and dotted
rhythms. (Pr, 1966, 2 pp.)

3.22 DIEMER, EMMA LOU. Gavotte.
Chords and melodies often built of fourths provide legato fingering practice. Marked "lively." Equal hand
emphasis. In 2/2. "Staccato touch in one hand, le-

gato touch in other hand." (B&H, 1962, 2 pp.) Fngr.
Anal.

3.23 DOLIN, SAMUEL. Old Dance (1953).
Haunting Andante semplice with skips in lovely melody.
Parallel seventh harmonies without third in section A,
included in section B; also double inflections of same
tone.   Legato double notes in LH, often parallel fifths.
In f aeolian mode. (In 8.1, 1 p.) MM. Biog.

3.24 DVORKIN, JUDITH. Castillano and Cubano.
How pleasant is the two-part Castillano! Marked
"lightly, with motion," its modernism lies in 5/8
meter, with melody usually grouped two plus three.
In A, no accidentals. Cubano has fluent motion in
four-measure phrases.   Traditional, except for constant alternation between 6/8 and 3/4.   Fast eighths
in the 6/8 measures. In G and e. Also in two parts,
RH leading. (In 2.3, 2 pp & 2 pp.) Fngr. Biog.

3.25 ELLIOTT, CARLETON. Three Alliterations.
March, Melancholy, and Mumbo-Jumbo are clean-cut
contemporary music, the character of each drawn with
confidence.   Textures of first and last pieces usually
in two voices.   Fluent and tonal March includes some
melodic and harmonic fourths.   Melancholy is depicted
by opposing dissonance and resolution of LH legato
fifths against RH octave-shifting ostinato of fifths.
Spontaneous Mumbo-Jumbo is great rhythmic fun.   At
beginning and end, LH uses ostinato figure in 5/8
while RH melody fitfully starts and stops.   Music begins and ends in d dorian mode, with last minute turn
to an A chord. (Wat, 1962, 5 pp.) Fngr, MM, Ped.
3 & 4.

3.26 FIALA, GEORGE. Lullaby.
Tender, skillfully written in flexible two-part texture.
Repeated four-measure fragment is sometimes melody,
sometimes acc.   Texture may be filled out with extra
part, providing LH legato double note practice. (BMI,
1958--also in 4.4, with Fngr, 2 pp.) MM.

3.27 FINE, VIVIAN. The Small Sad Sparrow.
Sensitive little two-part piece to be played "plaintive-
ly." Mostly in treble range, with upper part leading.
In phrygian mode on d, with some uncertainty. (In
4.1, 1 p.) Fngr, MM. Biog.

3.28 FINNEY, ROSS LEE.   There and Back, Berceuse,
      Skipping, and Reflections.
      These extracts (see also 4.46 and 4.47) from Finney's
      Inventions, first published in 1957.   (Remaining pieces
      from 1957 edition and new works are in Peters edition
      No. 6623, published in 1971.)   Showing fine creative
      flair, There and Back is invented from the obvious
      idea of ascending and descending motion, mostly in
      dotted rhythms.   Twelve-tone set used, twice forward,
      and twice retrograde (Back of the title).   One-line
      music.   Berceuse is a perfect little construction.
      Tone set heard, including transposition up half tone,
      with first tone of set used as a pedal point.   Fuller
      texture at end with sostenuto pedal and coupled writing.
      Melodic sense in Skipping is convincing.   Set used
      once forward and once backward.   Coupled writing in
      major thirds, much dotted note motion "in strict tem-
      po."   Ends with trill in both hands.   Reflections,
      strictly constructed, is surprisingly tuneful for twelve-
      tone music.   All motion between hands is contrary.
      Forearm staccato, two-note slurs.   (In 3.5, 1 p, 1/2
      p, 1/2 p, & 1 p.)   Fngr, some Ped.   *Biog.

3.29 FLEMING, ROBERT.   Strolling (1946).
      Lovely simplicity.   Most often in two voices, with LH
      acc adding gentle coloring of ninths, sevenths or sec-
      onds to folklike melody.   Acc has repeated two or
      three-measure patterns.   In aeolian mode on a.   (In
      8.1, 1 p.)   MM.   Biog.

3.30 FLETCHER, GRANT.   Marching Music for Johnny
      Appleseed.
      Entirely in bass range, music captures a rough vigour.
      In F mixolydian mode.   LH has hand or forearm
      strokes, which will strengthen weak fingers.   Fine dy-
      namic variety.   (Pr, 1957--also in 3.1, 2 pp.)   Fngr,
      MM.   *Anal.   Ch.

3.31 FREED, ISADORE.   Waltz on White Keys.
      Sophisticated music is fine introduction to mild disso-
      nance.   Lovely melody.   In pure dorian and aeolian
      modes, no black keys.   Provides practice for RH sing-
      ing legato and LH three-note chords.   (Pr, 1956--also
      in 3.1, 2 pp.)   Fngr.   *Anal.

3.32 GEORGE, JON.   A Day in the Jungle.
      These spontaneous works should delight children.

Titles, illustrations by the composer, and "lyrics"
are imaginative. Pianistically well planned. Covers
wide range. Usually one line to a hand. Four numbers use only bass range and four have ostinato LH
acc. "Teaching features of each piece are listed in
the Contents." Conservative. The pure D Elephant
Walking uses broken fourth ostinato acc. Gazelle
Prancing has exotic coloring from references to lydian
mode. Whole tone scale only in Tiger Stalking. Hands
move in contrary motion. Treble and bass alternate
for Baboons Talking. Has an augmented second. Ascending broken fifths and octaves depict Giant Vines
Growing. Out-of-key thirds indicate "its huge green
leaves are shimmering in the sun." (SB, 1968, 12
pp.) 12 pieces. Fngr, Ped. Anal. Ch. 3, some 2.

3.33 GIBBS, ALAN. Six Characters from Shakespeare.
Humorous characters particularly apt. Quotation included for each piece. Equal hand emphasis. Needs
very little pedal. Slight modernisms grafted on traditional tonal music. Neoclassic. Jolly Falstaff "rum-
bustiously" provides practice for two-voice texture of
varied and independent articulations. Harmonic fun,
such as sudden introduction of an A-flat chord after
much C, retention of only the E-flat, then B, next uncertainty, and C at end. Cordelia unified by repeated
acc figure and by some mirror motion. Played "sad-
ly." Tension is built in middle section by slow climb
after much tone repetition, texture thickened by voice
addition and inner voice activity. In Touchstone,
marked "scherzoso," fingering designed to strengthen
weak fingers. In C, no accidentals. Two-part texture
with hands equal. (Hin 424, 1966, 8 pp.) Fngr.

3.34 GIDEON, MIRIAM. Walk.
Many melodic and harmonic thirds in a conservative
idiom for this thoughtful Allegretto. Much cross relation and chromaticism. Treble range only. Usually
for two voices. (In 4.1, 1 p.) Fngr. Biog.

3.35 GREEN, RAY. March Sonatina No. 1.
Direct, simple tunes with leaps, mainly fourths, fifths,
and octaves. Offbeat acc, usually in LH, is second inversion triads or staccato sixths. In mixolydian mode
on A and C. RH repeated tones, using hand staccato.
MM must be half note equal to 100. Conservative.
(AME, 1956, 2 pp.) MM. Ch.

3.36 GREEN, RAY. Pieces for Children.
Spontaneous appeal. Works also suitable, as subtitle
suggests, "for grownups to make a note of." Much
coupled writing and syncopation. Harmonies used are
often "major-minor"--each of the pieces uses "either
the major or minor third of the scale." March has a
kind of rural energy. In main section, triad thirds
omitted. RH has fast repeated harmonic fourths using
hand staccato. Section B adds full triads in each hand.
Section C has coupled writing two octaves apart. In
Melody, direction to "ring out melody" reflects its
strong, open character. Many melodic fourths. LH
acc is like an ostinato; fourths again frequent, also
fifths. (AME, 1951, 9 pp.) 4 pieces. MM. *Anal.
3 & 4.

3.37 GREEN, RAY. Square Dance Sonatina.
"Energetic" high spirits with simple direct appeal.
One section "like a hoe down." C mixolydian mode,
with much back-and-forth LH offbeat acc, second in-
version tonic and minor dominant seventh chords.
(AME, 1956, 2 pp.) MM. Ch.

3.38 GREEN, RAY. Western Sky.
Pleasant, relaxed Allegretto in F. Some originality
in LH acc of broken inverted triads, or harmonic
sixths. Usually progressing by step, acc may be consonant or dissonant with melody. LH sixths use legato fingering. Jazz influence indicated by variable
third degree and final added sixth. Conservative.
(AME, 1958, 2 pp.) Some Fngr, Ped.

3.39 HEGEDÜS, ÁRPÁD. Flowers I Have Seen.
Sensitive and poetic. Chromaticism brings originality
amid tonal harmonies. Traditional rhythm. Mostly
homophonic texture. Why music has flower titles is
inexplicable. Charming illustrations by Lorraine
Blake. The carefree Andante Daisy has much dotted
rhythm. Clearly centered in lydian mode on F, with
numerous chromaticisms and polyharmonies. Motion
by fourths. In the Andante Tulip the two hands, each
having single part, seem oblivious to each other; but
when RH is transposed, LH also changes and both
cadence together in A. RH has broken thirds, LH has
tonic and dominant ostinato. (Oxf, 1965, 10 pp.) 5
pieces. MM. 3 & 4.

3. 40 HOPKINS, ANTHONY.   For Talented Beginners, Book
       II.
       Lively imaginative appeal.   Comments, in British ver-
       nacular, are fine help.   Modernisms slight.   Lovely
       Russian Song excellent for developing singing tone with
       weaker RH fingers, particularly since melody tone with
       chord has to match previous melody tone without chord.
       For Trumpets, "don't cling to the keys here--really
       have a go."   Excellent then, for freeing hand from key-
       board; also for developing strength with rapidly repeat-
       ed triads.   Sharp chordal jabs setting strings, un-
       damped by previous silent chords, in motion evoke
       Ghosts.   Busy is "a conventional exercise in fluency;
       get the joins between the hands smooth."   One-line
       music.   (Oxf, 1963, 11 pp.)   9 pieces.   Fngr.   Anal.

3. 41 HOVHANESS, ALAN.   Lullaby.
       Haunting Adagio in 6/8 traditional rhythms.   Uses
       familiar pentatonic mode simultaneously on white and
       black keys.   Simple treble melody accompanied by al-
       ternation between low tonic pedal point on D and much
       higher three-tone chords on black keys.   One brief
       section provides wonderful contrast.   (In 4.1, 1 p.)
       Fngr, MM, Ped.   Biog.

3. 42 HOVHANESS, ALAN.   Twelve Armenian Folk Songs,
       Op. 43.
       Settings are beautifully integrated with haunting, short-
       range melodies.   Often in dorian mode.   Clear phrases.
       LH octave reach.   Basic acc in II is interval of a
       fifth.   III in pure c dorian mode.   Beautiful six-tone
       melody omits characteristic raised sixth, but dronelike
       acc does use it.   Drone bass also interestingly varied
       in VIII.   Rhythm and melody more ornate in X than in
       others.   Compatibly, acc has florid sections.   Meter
       both 3/4 and 5/8.   Pure d phrygian mode.   In XII,
       melody emphasized with coupled writing (two octaves
       apart) for half its appearances.   Uses only tones in an
       exotic mode (like phrygian, but with raised fourth);
       augmented melodic second heard often.   (Pet 6432,
       1963, 10 pp.)   9 min.   MM.   *Anal.   3, some 4.

3. 43 JAQUE, RHENÉ.   The Little Grey Donkey.
       Awkward but gay.   Harmonic seconds stubbornly per-
       sist in acc, as well as short-long rhythm.   In lydian
       minor mode on g and e.   Some hand reversed posi-
       tions.   (GVT, 1968, 2 pp.)   MM.   Ch.

3.44 JOACHIM, OTTO. 12 Twelve-Tone Pieces for Children.
Childlike pieces depict titles with imagination. Twelve-tone writing easily apparent. All four set transformations printed. Set used in transpositions and segment repetitions, among other ways. First four tones of set make incomplete minor ninth chord, and last five complete minor ninth chord, indicating traditional harmony. Often a particular sonority heard repeatedly. Varied and sometimes extreme ranges explored. Last three numbers have imitation and canon, and use same subject. Very little octave reach. Poetic Bless You (good pedal study) has ostinato harmonic acc from first four tones of set. Mood is evoked in Full Moon by RH ostinato of harmonic seconds and fifths, while LH has infrequent color tones. Pedal held throughout. Descriptive Snowy Morning also has ostinato divided between hands while either hand catches long color tones. For Plastic Soldier (also in 3.2) retrograde form of set yields melody beginning like "taps." Octaves and major seconds used in this fast march. Allegro, staccato Gossip is portrayed by each hand having almost the same rhythm. (BMI, 1961, 15 pp.) Fngr, Ped. Ch. 3 & 4.

3.45 KARKOFF, MAURICE. Sex Små Pianostycken.
Six Small Pieces just right for early, easy exploration of contemporary music. Clear musical intentions in works of character. Keys with three flats and four sharps; also modal pieces. Four works have two-part texture. Titles in Swedish, German, and English. In the Andante Carillon hands alternate between three-tone chords (some added-note) and melody tones. 3/2 meter. Some polyharmonies. Jolly and accessible Rural Dance has delightful variety of tone inflections, such as play between lydian and aeolian mode on E-flat. Fine for dynamic contrasts. Punch's Dancing is an Allegro scherzando in E mixolydian mode. Bass has traditional waltz pattern, sometimes moving chromatically. RH has hand staccato and LH downward arm thrusts. (Geh, 1953, 6 pp.) 6 min, 9 sec. Fngr, MM, Ped. Ch. 3, some 4.

3.46 KAY, ULYSSES. Ten Short Essays.
Childlike and genuinely musical. Numerous uncommon rhythmic subtleties. Only a few octaves. Little pedal needed. Conservative approach to modern idiom. So

Gay is an Allegretto in C. Has a fling of four rapid
sixteenths. Rhythmic alertness needed for irregular
offbeat acc. Hands alternate in importance. Dynamic
variety. Tender Thought an introspective Andantino
with three-measure phrases. In aeolian mode. Acc
has inner voice, usually in LH, requiring finger change
for legato. In Old Lament melody is doubled with outside fingers. Acc often long thumb tones. Slumber
Song is a lovely singing Andantino. In E mixolydian
mode with puzzling color ending. Acc, alternating between hands, has complicated rhythm. March Song
has melodic and harmonic fourths and fifths to express
sturdiness. Equal hand emphasis, with acc hand often
having fifths on last half beat in 2/2 meter. (MCA,
1965, 11 pp.) Fngr, MM, Ped. Ch. 3, some 4.

3.47 KELEMEN, MILKO. The Donkey Walks Along the
      Beach.
      Serious works. Usually no concessions to easy ac-
      cess, despite appealing titles for children. The five
      or six faster works are easiest to grasp. No peda-
      gogical aims apparent; emphasis on fine music. Titles
      also in German and Serbo-Croatian. The Cricket Tunes
      Its Violin is apt and amusing with jaunty melody.
      Staccato minor seconds for cricket and fifths and near-
      fifths for violin's four strings. In the Adagio When
      Will the Swallows Come, two, three and four-tone
      combinations savored for sound, disregarding disso-
      nance or consonance. Largely non-tonal, but E-flat
      is repeated. Dancing Blades of Grass has graceful
      LH melody, sometimes coupled by RH. Dance is a
      waltz with RH offbeat intervals of thirds and fourths.
      The Bicyclist speeds rapidly by in one-line music,
      with two-note slurs alternating between hands. Ap-
      pears atonal. (Lit/Pet 5813, 1963, 9 pp.) 9 pieces.
      Fngr, MM, Ped. 3, some 4.

3.48 KHACHATURIAN, ARAM. Enfantines, No. 2.
      For Children, No. 2 is a pleasing legato study in which
      broken triads flow between alternating hands. Legato
      double notes in each hand. Much interchange between
      parallel major and minor. Treble range only. Con-
      servative. (In 5.2, 2 pp.) Fngr, MM, Ped.

3.49 KOHS, ELLIS B. Forlane.
      Introspective and dignified. Lyric nature gives chance
      to savor dissonant harmonies, starting from major and

minor used simultaneously.   LH acc often legato harmonic thirds.   (Mer, 1958, 2 pp.)   Fngr, MM.

3.50 KONOWITZ, BERT.   Choo-Choo Stomp.
Sturdy and nonchalant.   Indication is to "chug along:"
certainly LH does that with walking bass of constant
detached single notes.   RH melody often has short-long
rhythms.   Fourth is often raised, seventh lowered.
Final chord has added seventh, no third.   (LR, 1964,
2 pp.)   Fngr.

3.51 KONOWITZ, BERT.   Poundin' the Beat.
Spontaneous.   RH melody, moderately varied, uses
hand or finger staccato.   LH ostinato, related to boogie,
is major or minor broken triads.   (LR, 1962, 2 pp.)
Fngr.

3.52 KURKA, ROBERT.   Mid-Summer Day Dream and In a
      Cavern.
First title expressed by color chords at end of each of
the four-measure phrases.   Three voices (RH has only
sixths) easily move in and out of dissonant chords.   In
a Cavern, useful for smooth pianissimo touch with all
fingers, has coupled writing four octaves apart.   In f-
sharp.   Chromatic.   (Weint, 1960, 1 p & 1 p.)

3.53 LAKNER, YEHOSHUA.   Corner Stones.
Useful studies for developing hand independence.   For
serious student whose music doesn't have to be immediately attractive.   Preface explains that "this series of
19 studies was conceived as exercises in two-part writing in imitation style."   Hands usually take turns leading.   Earlier numbers often have lines inverted; double
counterpoint found.   Ranges are narrow, with little
necessity for thumb-under position.   Both tonal and
modal.   Key signatures usually omitted.   Flats more
in evidence, up to four used.   Rhythms are traditional,
although one piece uses 5/4.   Several notated with half
note as beat.   Programmatic titles not apt.   (IMP,
1961, 10 pp.)   Fngr.   3, some 2 & 4.

3.54 LA MONTAINE, JOHN.   Questioning.
Much imagination.   Title illustrated by indecision between flatted tone and unflatted tone an octave lower.
Usually one line only, hands alternating.   Fine dynamic
variety.   Many minor thirds.   (Oxf, 1964--also in 2.3,
1 p.)   Fngr, MM.   Biog.

3.55 LANTIER, MAURICE. Ping-Pong.
Spontaneous. Hand alternation and harmonic seconds
depict the title. Useful for forearm staccatos. Conservative. (In 3.6, 1 p.) Ch.

3.56 LEVY, MARVIN DAVID. O-'Matsuri.
These "Five easy piano pieces for children," titled
The Festival, are fun with a tasteful purity. In keys
of C, F, and G--no accidentals. Many added-note
chords. Pianistically consistent. Imaginative stories
and colorful illustrations from Japanese life included.
The Dragonfly Hunt, marked "lightly," is graceful.
Teasingly traditional, yet not traditional; for instance,
last two measures have tonic harmony, but sixth scale
step is in melody and there is added second at end--
also short-long rhythm. Insect Concert needs finger
changes on held tones for legato double notes. (B&H,
1966, 5 pp.) 5 pieces. Ch.

3.57 LOMBARDO, ROBERT. Twelve Contemporary Pieces
for Children.
Splendid in musical integrity, these quiet, dignified
pieces require sensitivity. In foreword composer
writes: "These children's pieces differ from most other compositions of their kind in that they are written
in a contrapuntal style. Also, they employ for the
most part phrase lengths other than those of four or
eight bars and unlike most children's pieces the tonal
material used is not triadic." Concerning "a contrapuntal style" there is usually one principal melody.
May be two parts only; a third or fourth part may be
added for sonority. No key signatures, and usually no
more than two sharps or one flat. Little pedal needed
--ranges are moderate. While titles are for children,
music suitable for any age. Old Wooden Stairs has
gracefully curved melody. Ending indicates E as tonic,
with added second and fourth. Lullaby is in G, ending
just short of the tonic. Principal material is first in
RH, then repeated in LH. The Silver Box has double
notes which need fingering change on held tones and
pedal for legato. Clowning is spontaneous with surprise
rests and meter changes. (Peer, 1966, 12 pp.) MM.
Ch.

3.58 McKAY, GEORGE FREDERICK. Explorations, Vol. 1.
Subtitled "an introduction to modern music"; fortunately,
intent is not too educational, and so spontaneity wins out

over too orderly illustrations.   Informative preface.
A Western Ballad has single line treble melody accompanied by infrequent double notes.   Chorale has four-
tone legato chords--"triads in varied relation to root
tones"--so final phrase has progression of a, f-sharp,
a, c, e-flat, and F triads.   Lolly-Too-Toodum-Ti-O
and Phantom Cry show the variety of expression found
in collection: former is naive and latter sophisticated-
ly expressionistic; former uses coupled writing in
tenths and latter is fragmented and atonal.   (JF 9638,
1962, 16 pp.)   12 pieces.   Anal.   3, some 2.

3.59 McKAY, GEORGE FREDERICK.   Dance in the Meadow.
Allegro of zest has fine bounce, using both legato and
staccato touches.   In D mixolydian mode.   Fourth
chords and seventh chords in dissonant arrangement.
(Pr, 1965--also in 3.61, 2 pp.)   Fngr, MM.

3.60 McKAY, GEORGE FREDERICK.   Dance Pastorale
         (Rondino).
As basic as a folk dance.   Direction "gaily" describes
mood.   Tonal; some G mixolydian mode.   Hands alternate in activity and exchange roles.   RH weak fingers
are exercised.   Five-finger passages.   (Pr, 1957--
also in 3.1, 2 pp.)   Fngr.   *Anal.

3.61 McKAY, GEORGE FREDERICK.   Seven Outdoor Pieces.
Three works reviewed.   (See 2.35 and 3.59.)   Others
are too conservative for this Guide.   Navajo Lullaby
is graceful, naturally flowing tone study.   Equal hand
emphasis.   Main section uses a pentatonic mode, but
with extra tone of f-sharp highlighted.   Acc includes
legato, harmonic fourths.   (Pr, 1967, 14 pp.)   Some
Fngr.   3, some 2.

3.62 MARTINON, JEAN.   The Ballad of the Unbreakable
         Soldier.
Bright, "decisive" sounds capture picture of ramrod-
straight soldier; unusual leaps portray toy's rigidity.
Adventurous harmony.   Clear G, from much reitera-
tion of tonic tone, but all twelve tones freely used.
Hand staccato.   Lower clef of last system, second
measure, should be treble.   (In 3.6, 1 p.)   Fngr,
MM.   Ch.

3.63 MASSIAS, GÉRARD.   Alice au Pays des Merveilles
         (1948).

Delightfully apt settings of quotations in French from
Alice in Wonderland. Music truly childlike, without
condescension. Melodies, with individual twists of
mildly contemporary flavor, are particularly appealing.
Textures mostly thin. Ranges fairly wide. Collection
a fine start with contemporary music, because tonal
works are conservative. In Alice's Garden (I), marked
"moderate and dreamy," has repeated bass pattern
(taken up by treble for an ending) depicting Alice's
boredom. Change between 9/8 and 3/4 uses duplet
and triplet. Skillful chromatic shifts. The Mouse's
Sad Tale (III) is poignant in its simplicity. Phrygian
mode on e. Acc, alternating between hands, uses only
parallel staccato (forearm) thirds. Trial of the Queen
of Hearts (VII) describes serious court scene with dissonant fanfare introduction. Soon, as Alice grows to
normal size, action becomes fast as Alice tells the
people: "You're nothing but a pack of cards." Much
use for hand staccato. Material from first number repeated to depict Alice waking from her dream. Translations are The White Rabbit (II) and "bantering," A
Mad Tea Party (IV), Waltz of the Duchess (V), and
Round of the Crocodile (VI). (Bil, 1968, 14 pp.) 7
pieces. MM. Ch. 3, some 4.

3.64 MOORE, DOUGLAS. Decoration Day and Mississippi.
Decoration Day has fine early American style in its
rollicking 6/8 tune "in swinging march time." Triad
outlines in RH melody. Acc has forearm staccato
thirds. Different articulation in each hand. Mississippi, in two distinct parts, has authentic ring. The
first has "slow and sad" melody in coupled writing in
pentatonic mode; spontaneous second section in A is
"more lively," like a cakewalk. Material of each section repeated, the first being set with RH counter melody using repeated tones. Whole ends ff. (In 3.4,
2 pp & 2 pp.) Fngr. *Biog.

3.65 MOORE, DOUGLAS. Escalator and The Princess and
       the Pea.
Escalator is delightful and useful. RH syncopated melody has fourths and fifths. LH perpetual motion acc
is splendid etude because of ostinato four-note ascending figures using weaker fingers and contractions.
Two voices. In c aeolian mode--no accidentals. Second piece is "a drowsy waltz" with graceful melodic
profile. Tonal, but with piquant nonharmonic tones.

LH acc has legato thirds, also practice in reaching for
lower bass tones. (In 3.5, 1 p & 2 pp.) Fngr, some
Ped. *Biog. 3 & 4.

3.66 NORDOFF, PAUL. The Fourth Sings.
Lovely, natural music. Melody sings, as well as
many closely intertwined accompanying harmonic fourths.
Lyric treble line is not commonplace, yet not in the
least esoteric. In F. Second inversion triads between
the hands. Conservative. (AME, 1965, 2 pp.)

3.67 OKUMURA, HAJIME. Japanese Children's Songs for
Piano.
Melodies often very beautiful, complemented by com-
patible settings. Several melodies use familiar pentatonic mode; two others use a pentatonic mode with
two half steps, another uses one half step; one piece
uses pentatonic mode for entire fabric. Two melodies
use only four tones. Three works are in treble range,
as are parts of others. Two use two sharps, others
fewer sharps or flats. Practice for three-tone chords
with added second. Octaves used. Titles in Japanese
and English. Notes in Japanes for all pieces, in
English for ten. You're a Good Boy (p 5) has two
phrases twice, as well as an introduction and ending.
New Year is Coming (p 6) has unusual variety, such
as coupled writing with additional acc or florid LH
acc. Characteristic tritone used. Come on Through
(p 15) has koto-influenced alternation of melody and
acc, excellent for rotary motion. Grass for the Goat
(p 17), from Okinawa, has another tritone, and legato
thirds in LH setting. Mr. Moon, How Old Are You? (p 21)
is bimodal, using for LH acc purely pentatonic mode
on black keys. Legato octaves in acc require endurance. In Where Are You From? (p 24) brilliance is accumulated by repetition of dotted rhythm.
Texture works up to six-tone chords. (Ongaku, 1964,
24 pp.) 14 pieces. Fngr, MM; Ch. 3 & 4, some
5.

3.68 OSBORNE, WILLSON. Contrasts.
Fascinating melody has memorable turning-on-itself
quality. Title comes from variety of range, mode,
and speed. Section A uses treble range, dorian mode
on f-sharp and Andante con moto tempo; section B
uses bass range, aeolian mode on e and has a faster
tempo. LH uses little more than two chords. 2/2,

3/2, 3/4, and 5/4 meters. (Pr, 1954, 2 pp.) Fngr,
MM.

3.69 OSBORNE, WILLSON. Puppet Dance.
Carefree Allegro vivace. Melody has lively non-legato
patter of repeated tones; acc has repetitive, detached
chords. In mixolydian mode. (Pr, 1954, 2 pp.)
Fngr, MM.

3.70 PAPINEAU-COUTURE, JEAN. Aria.
Well integrated, undemonstrative Modéré in two voices.
LH acc more active than RH. Interval of fourth much
used in sequential LH. Twelve-tone. (BMI, 1964, 2
pp.) Fngr.

3.71 PENTLAND, BARBARA. Echoes
Jolly works are "2 pieces for young pianists with shifting 5-finger positions." Echoes II reverses role of
hands from Echoes I. In Echoes I, LH presses down
a chord and holds it without sounding, while RH
prances around with a "hard staccato." Often RH
crosses over held chord. Faster two-note slurs and
short-long rhythms used. (WAT, 1968, 1 p & 1 p.)
Fngr. Ch.

3.72 PERLE, GEORGE. Interrupted Story (1956).
Fascinating adventure of graceful melodic interest.
Deft rhythmic, harmonic, and dynamic variety. Octave
reaches. (Pr, 1957, 2 pp.) Fngr. *Anal.

3.73 PERSICHETTI, VINCENT. Parades, Op. 57.
Musically uncomplicated pieces of infectious gaiety,
usually f and more in dynamics. March has splendidly
festive air from freely associated triads (some polyharmony), dotted rhythms and staccato scales. Allegretto Canter tuneful with modal shifts. Pomp, marked
Allegro con brio, has audacious polyharmonies from
broken chord melodies and root position triads in acc.
(EV, 1955, 6 pp.) 3 pieces. MM, Ped. Ch.

3.74 PERSICHETTI, VINCENT. Piano Sonatinas 1-6.
First three earlier sonatinas are noticeably more difficult than last three. Sonatina No. 2, Op. 45 (in one
movement has sure grasp of mercurial and dissonant
tonal harmony. Counterpoint important throughout the
two sections. Slower severe opening section is a canon,
where the imitation involves double notes. Longer sec-

tion, twice as fast as opening, is hilarious, mixing
athletic finger exercise, jazz, and polyharmony. Canon
reintroduced in quieter part; later an augmentation of
opening double notes. Sonatina No. 3, Op. 47 (in two
movements) has masterful contemporary tonal music,
attractive and individual. First slow movement marked
"warmly and singing." Leading RH melody always un-
folding like an arabesque, with little noticeable repetition. Continuous-motion acc, anchored on pedal tone,
gradually ascends while momentarily visiting several
modes. In two-voice texture. Graceful faster second
movement, marked "brightly," has articulation interest. Excellent practice for double notes in each hand.

Last three Sonatinas are often delightfully naive, although not for children alone. Melodies usually diatonic. Moderate chromaticism in tonal harmonies;
harmonies often move in parallel motion. Traditional
rhythms and textures. Sonatina 4, Op. 63 has three
movements; 5, Op. 64 has two movements; and 6, Op.
65, one movement. In Op. 63, opening Allegretto is
based on five-finger melody alternating between hands.
Legato double note acc. Key is C, but keys like B
visited. In the Andantino, when RH broken triad melody is repeated half step higher, accompanying parallel thirds remain at same pitch. Acc uses finger exchange for legato. In the closing Moderato a fragment
of the treble melody, on one triad, is harmonized by
as many as four different descending broken seventh
chords. (EV, 1957, 30 pp.) MM. 3, 4, 5, & 6.

3.75 PERSICHETTI, VINCENT. Serenade No. 7, Op. 55.
Refreshingly unsophisticated, probably best for children, but also appealing to older children-at-heart.
Opportunities for finger legato. Uses only two octaves. Walk has melody using different five-finger
positions. Contrast between phrygian and dorian modes
on a. In Play quickly alternating hands bring into
juxtaposition cross relations, which sometimes sound
together. Much accelerando with crescendo, then return to tempo. Sleep, more tender, starts in G-flat,
slowly drifts downward chromatically, and partially
returns. LH acc is notated slow trill. (EV, 1957,
10 pp.) 6 pieces. MM, Ped. Ch. 3, some 4.

3.76 POOT, MARCEL. In All Directions.
Attractive, sometimes humorous collection shows folk

influences from England, France, Spain, and Russia.
Modernisms are mild--complex cluster chords the
most prevalent. Texture always RH melody and LH
acc. Tempos range from Allegretto to faster. Two
tunes in rollicking 6/8 meter. Keys used are C, G,
a, and e. No reach beyond seventh. Although subtitled "a collection of pieces for the young pianist,"
this music suitable for all ages. On the Spanish Bor-
der economically captures Bolero allure. In a minor
with varied inflections of sixth and seventh steps. Allegro violento From Omsk to Tomsk humorously bears
out its title through jabbing ff cluster chords. Meter
changes arouse attention. (UE 13828, 1965, 10 pp.)
5 pieces. Fngr. 3, some 4.

3.77 POOT, MARCEL. Petite Marche.
"Solid" and attractive Little March offers much keyboard experience: (a) coupled writing one and two octaves apart, (b) two and three-tone chords, including
fourth chords, (c) melody and acc reversed between
hands, (d) forearm staccato, and (e) brief imitation.
In d and F. (In 5.2, 2 pp.) Fngr, MM. Ch.

3.78 RATTALINO, PIERO. Otto Pezzi per Fanciulli (1964).
These very musical Eight Small Pieces for Children
are highly recommended; also suitable for adults.
Have prominent contemporary techniques at an easy
level. Much two-part texture, sometimes with imitation. Some coupled writing. No key signatures. 3
has unexpected chromatic acc tones, but repetitive,
plainer melody more elemental. 6 is a beauty, with
mildly jagged contemporary melody and lovely dissonant harmonies. Largely non-tonal. Lento 7 is like
Hindemith in rhythms of double dotted note followed by
two short notes and in interval structure of fourths and
fifths. In the fanciful Vivace 8, single tones are isolated, as in Webern, by extreme ranges and rests.
One section more traditional. Suggestions of both
twelve-tone and tonal writing. (Zer, 1965, 7 pp.)
Some Fngr. 3 & 4.

3.79 RICCARDI, JOSEPH. Little Prelude.
Splendidly consistent. Fine for pedal study--some
tones need none. In pure phrygian on e, except for
two f-sharps. LH acc consists of ascending or descending three-tone broken chords, composed of root,
fifth, and root. Usually small-interval lateral shifts

for each hand. (Pr, 1964, 2 pp.) Fngr, Ped.

3.80 RICCARDI, JOSEPH. The Lonely Swan.
Poignant. Technically consistent, with simple explorations beyond five-finger position; LH reaches low for
first-beat tones, but has only two positions. RH singing melody. Tonal, but key is vague. (EV, 1964, 2
pp.) Ch.

3.81 RICHMAN, ALICE. Clowning.
Lovely composition, convincing in its consistent pianism. Varies between a aeolian and C--uses only white
keys. Except for clear lateral changes, lines usually
encompass only a sixth. RH has only melody tones.
LH has a few three-tone chords. Considerable independence between hands. (Pr, 1965, 2 pp.) Some
Fngr, MM. Ch.

3.82 RICKER, EARL. Escape to Sherwood.
This breathless escape accomplished musically "with
driving energy." Program included. Polyharmonies
with almost exclusive use of triads in root position.
Changes between 3/4 and 2/4. Technically valuable.
Triads are either harmonic, broken with staccato
(hand) single and double notes, or all single notes.
(LR, 1967, 2 pp.) Fngr, MM.

3.83 RIDOUT, ALAN. Fun & Games.
Most musical. Titles well depicted. Variety between
vigorous pieces and quiet works of interesting originality. Tonal, some modal. Interpretative maturity required of child performer. Apt comments for performance. Vivace Football, in ABA form, is spontaneous. A has broken triads which total up to ninth and
eleventh chords--or perhaps the subdominant over tonic
final chord indicates a polychordal analysis. B has
mirror writing. Fine for forearm staccatos. Grazioso Sailing has noteworthy harmonization. While treble
melody is clearly in aeolian, LH four-note semi-ostinato includes lowered tonic. Adagio misterioso mood
in Ghosts skillfully aroused by chromatic melody over
bass open fifths. Pedal blurs melody tones. Friendly
Fight pits LH black keys against RH white keys.
Strengthens all fingers. Much offbeat acc. Tree
Climbing has lovely flow. In two voices, with much
contrary motion. "Here you could easily be let down
by your fingering, so be careful especially towards the

end of the piece, when you near the topmost branch."
Thumb-under practice. (St&B, 1962, 17 pp.) 10
pieces. Fngr. Anal. Ch.

3.84 RIDOUT, ALAN. Fun & Games I.
Genuinely childlike and appealing. Modernisms should
not present problems. Many pieces are modal, including two in lochrian. Several use half-note for unit.
Pianistically consistent: about half are in five-finger
positions; none stray far. Three have contrary motion. Very few double notes. Ten pieces are either
in all treble or all bass. Imaginative comments stem
from programmatic titles and may include simple
pianistic observation. The Campfire is gentle. In
pure b lochrian. LH ostinato outlines b triad. RH
has two-note slurs. The Castle marked largo, is ma-
jestic because of bass register and repeated harmonic
fifths and fourths. Cowboy uses familiar pentatonic
mode on black keys. LH has traditional 6/8 ostinato
rhythm, with tones based on the dominant. Fireworks
has brilliant loud stabs of seconds and percussive fifths
with added seconds. Develops strength and endurance
with rapid forearm staccatos. Seagulls proceeds unob-
trusively by canon at the sixth. The Spaceship is realistic. "Spaceships make hardly any noise--except for
their clear signals." Signals are irregular treble
peeps of major and minor seconds. Tonal, but not
concerned with exact key. The lively Tag has energetic RH hand staccatos and LH two-note slurs. In e
phrygian. (Note well collection title here and that for
3.83.) (St&B, 1963, 18 pp.) 20 pieces. Fngr.
Anal. Ch. 3, some 2.

3.85 ROGERS, ELIZABETH. Knight in Armor.
"Scowling fiercely" most certainly, rough medieval
mood masterfully manifested. Staccato fifths on both
white and black keys move by steps, clashing uncouth-
ly with each other. Some mirror motion. Develops
strength. F mixolydian mode. (LR, 1962, 2 pp.)
Fngr. Ch.

3.86 SCHMIDT, Y. RUDNER. A Caminho da Escola (1967).
Allegro School Path has lovely treble sounds. Melody's
regular phrases quickly ascend with all fingers. Simple syncopations. Traditional LH acc moves back and
forth with seconds as bright dissonances. Piece ends
in B-flat, made sure in only the short middle section.

Final tonic triad includes added second and sixth. (IVi,
1968, 2 pp.) Fngr, Ped.

3.87 SCHMIDT, Y. RUDNER. A Canção do Negrinho (1967).
Song of the Little Black Boy has a lovely treble melody.
Marked "gentle," in two voices, its treble LH acc often has syncopation of habanera rhythm, with tone tied
through beginning of second beat. Delicate chromatic
coloring. Fine tone study. (IVi, 1968, 2 pp.) Fngr.

3.88 SCHRAMM, HAROLD. Jàvali.
Perfect little work, aims and results convincingly balanced. Jàvali is "a love song based on a compositional style popular in India." Melodies covering a fifth
waver between major, melodic minor with usual changes
often reversed, and lydian mode. Hands alternate on
melody. (Pr, 1966, 2 pp.) Fngr, MM.

3.89 SHAPERO, HAROLD. Song Without Words (1956).
Melody really sings. Acc has either LH repeated
chords or active, RH lovely counter melody. Very
conservative. (Pr, 1957, 2 pp.) Fngr, MM. *Anal.

3.90 SHAPERO, HAROLD. Staccato Dance.
Spontaneous and good-natured. RH needs agility in
scales. LH uses only forearm staccato broken octaves with some skips. Conservative. (Pr, 1957, 2
pp.) Fngr, MM. *Anal.

3.91 SHOSTAKOVICH, D. Histoire Gaie.
Allegro Gay Story is immediately appealing. Music
moves momentarily among keys such as e and A-flat.
Equal hand emphasis. Much hand alternation as well
as coupled writing. Forearm staccatos, often on brok-
en triads. Medium wide range. (In 5.2, 2 pp.) Fngr.

3.92 SHULMAN, ALAN. Dripping Faucet and March.
Realistic Dripping Faucet has irregular hand alternation and spasmodic rests. Fine for economical hand
staccato. March, marked "springy," has effective
rhythmic interest, with irregular accents in RH melody
against steady LH chords. Chords a half step, "too
high" substitute for the usual. (Wein, 1960, 1 p & 2
pp.) MM. 3 & 4.

3.93 SHULMAN, ALAN. Lopsided.
Whimsically depicts title. Impression of disproportion

is attained by 5/8 meter, melody trying to group itself by four eighths, and ostinato acc attempting the
same. Melodic phrases interrupted by polychords.
(Wein, 1960, 3 pp.) MM.

3.94 STARER, ROBERT. Bugle, Drum and Fife.
Fine march tempo. Triplets between hands and in one
hand mixed with eighths and sixteenths. Often brightly
polytonal. Wide spacing sometimes. No chords. (Pr,
1956, 2 pp.) Fingr. *Anal.

3.95 STEIN, LEON. Holiday.
"Buoyant," colorful piece with "strong modulations."
Pianistically useful for (a) LH rocking chord acc cov-
ering a ninth, (b) coupled five-finger passages, and
(c) RH legato double notes. (Mer, 1957, 2 pp.) Fngr.
*Anal.

3.96 STERNKLAR, AVRAHAM. Bamidbar in the Desert.
Desert atmosphere created in consistent Allegro ritmico. In Hungarian minor scale on D, except raised
sixth step brings augmented second to scale. Two
slurred tones ending staccato and acc syncopation are
characteristic rhythms. (Pr, 1965, 2 pp.) Fngr.

3.97 STERNKLAR, AVRAHAM. A Brisk March.
Appealing work with interesting dotted notes and triplets combined in melody. Harmonic fifths in acc,
sometimes with added fourth. Mixolydian mode on G,
some dorian on f. Wide range. (Pr, 1964, 2 pp.)
Fngr.

3.98 STERNKLAR, AVRAHAM. Flute Song.
Ancient-sounding Allegretto in dorian mode on d.
Flutelike melody is very high for main strain, acc line
low. In central section offbeat acc in middle range.
Finger legato on repeated tones. Discreet pedal can
aid broken octave reaches. (CF, 1962, 2 pp.) Fngr.

3.99 STEVENS, EVERETT. Tunes in Folk Style.
These modal tunes have lovely simplicity of folk songs.
Modality sometimes briefly abandoned for tonality.
Settings usually have three tones, LH using many har-
monic fifths. Tunes are excellent for developing sense
of phrase contour. I is in f-sharp phrygian mode.
Melody omits fifth tone. II uses a pentatonic mode,
melody using only black keys. Played "gaily and fast."

"Lively" IV is also pentatonic, using only white keys.
(Dit, 1956, 3 pp.) 6 pieces. Fngr. 3 & 4.

3.100 STEVENS, HALSEY. Jumping Colts (1961).
Spontaneous Allegretto, bounding wonderfully between
hands, is essentially one-line music. Acc is intermittent staccato strokes. Jagged melody line. Centered
on D, with as many as two sharps or two flats; mixolydian mode prominent. Rhythmically straightforward.
(Hel, 1968, 4 pp.) 1 min. MM.

3.101 STEVENS, HALSEY. Lyric Piece (1955).
Andante con moto of haunting beauty. Tonal in a thoroughly contemporary and appealing way. Legato double
notes need sensitive chordal balance. Short-long
rhythm. (Mer, 1956, 2 pp.) MM. *Anal.

3.102 STEVENS, HALSEY. Music for Ann (1952-53).
Fine workmanship, suitable for adults also. Three
works in 2/2. Very few sharps or flats. Sober Prelude in two nearly equal voices. Modal influences.
Lovely Quiet Song in 5/4 and 3/4. Hands change
flexibly between melody with prominent broken chords
and acc of legato double notes. In D. Jaunty Piece
for Skipping has changing meters and forearm staccatos. Very flexibly tonal. (Hel, 1960, 10 pp.) 5
pieces. 5 min, 30 sec. Some Fngr. Ch.

3.103 SZABÓ, FERENC. Preludium and Scherzo.
What lovely wayward application of familiar tonal materials in Preludium! Frequent dissonance to conso-
nance and V-I progressions provide freshness. Melodies dip unexpectedly to real resting places. Texture
is melody/acc. RH has legato thirds. Scherzo has
folklike treble dance tune which sometimes has two-
note slurs contrary to constant 2/4 patter. Opportunity
for LH rapid wrist work with staccato back-and-forth
action between fifth and first fingers. In pure d dorian mode. (In 4.8, 1 p & 1 p.) Fngr.

3.104 SZELÉNYI, ISTVÁN. Forty Short Piano Pieces for
Beginners, Book 2.
(See 1.5 for general remarks.) 5/8 meters, changing
meters, and successive beats divided by two, three,
four, and five are added to those in Book 1 (see 2.48).
Ballad has "speaking" bass melody with many repeated
tones. 5/8 meter, three-measure phrases. Like a

Szekeley Ballad has haunting "speaking" melody with infrequent beautiful color chords.   Second section has
melody repeated in coupled texture and ff dynamics.
At the Playground bounces joyfully and rapidly from
hand to hand.   In d, with interesting accidentals, including a-flat.   Rugged strength in Wild Czardas, provided by ff stabs, pounding bass, rapid two-note slurs,
and short-long rhythms.   In Hungarian minor scale on
C, with much f-sharp.   Whoopee is great title for high-
spirited work.   Strong forearm staccatos used for
scalar melody and broken fifth acc.   In lydian minor
scale.   (Above pieces also in 1.5.)   At the Brook has
irresistible tune.   Fingers changed on repeated tones
to increase the range.   Acc always a tremolo in
thirds.   Material exchanged between the hands.   Melody of Request has unusual chromaticism.   Excellent
for measuring note values from a half through a sixteenth, and for finger legato on repeated tones.   (EMB,
1957, 18 pp.)   20 pieces.   Fngr.   3, some 4 & 5.

3.105 SZOKOLAY, SÁNDOR.   Teasing and Tom Thumb.
In Teasing B vexes B-flat, E plagues E-flat.   Andante
sostenuto also rivals Allegro.   Accent, staccato, and
tenuto add variety.   Double notes in LH.   Tom Thumb,
briskly accented, has fine diversity, such as play between f and lydian mode, and shifts in tempo from nonchalant Allegretto to expressive rubato to Vivace.
Chords alternate rapidly between hands and acc is intricate offbeat.   (In 4.8, 1/2 p & 2 pp.)   Ch.   3 & 4.

3.106 TANSMAN, ALEXANDER.   Chromatics (1954).
Attractive lyrical number, marked "moderately and very
smooth."   Mostly in two voices, RH leading.   LH descends chromatically, and has broken octaves.   Conservative.   (In 3.3, 1 p.)   Fngr.   *Biog.

3.107 TARDOS, BÉLA.   Jest.
Rough fun comes from added fifth beat with "false"
tone; other dissonances, syncopations and relentless
open fifths further the mood.   A Moderato con ritmo in
C.   (In 4.8, 1/2 p.)   Fngr.   Ch.

3.108 TCHEREPNIN, ALEXANDER.   Chimes (1954).
Realistic, big sound, attained in part by holding damper
pedal.   To be played "vigorously and well marked."
Many melodic and harmonic fourths and fifths.   Repeated tones and RH rotary motion.   (In 3.3, 2 pp.)

Fngr, Ped.   *Biog.

3.109 TCHEREPNIN, ALEXANDER. Hide and Seek.
Bright little work, to be played "with spirit." Explores
wide keyboard range. Hand or forearm staccato brok-
en octaves. Equal hand emphasis. Usually pp. (In
3.4, 1 p.) Fngr, Ped. *Biog. Ch.

3.110 VANIER, JEANNINE. Five Pieces for Children.
Moderately contemporary, gentle works use varied
techniques. Three in mixolydian mode. Texture is
predominantly melody and two or three-tone chordal
acc. Titles also in French. Lisette's Mirror in two-
part mirror and double counterpoint. My Sleigh Goes
too Fast an Allegro moderato with five-finger passage
work for both hands. Legato fourths and fifths for
acc. Dance is dignified like an old gavotte, in e aeolian mode, played Allegro moderato. Middle section
has imitation in two voices. Articulation varied and
effective. (Wat, 1960, 5 pp.) Fngr, some MM. Ch.
3 & 4.

3.111 VAN SLYCK, NICHOLAS. In Two Parts.
Ingenious Moderato of splendid craftsmanship. Straightforward D melody is accompanied by second part of
considerable note freedom, emphasizing four-note motive. Equal treatment for each hand. Wide range.
(In 2.3, 1 p.) Fngr. Biog.

3.112 WATSON, SCOTT. March of the Moon Folk.
Tread of imaginary people comes from acc parallel
harmonic seconds. Final polychord directly confirms
incipient polyharmony throughout. Valuable for teaching equality between hands, wide keyboard exploration
and forearm and hand staccatos. (Row, 1967, 2 pp.)
Fngr. Ch.

3.113 WAXMAN, DONALD. The Brass Band Begins.
Descriptive fun. Players begin together for two phrases,
then basses lose their way, panic, stop, and confuse the
treble players into ending on the dominant. Four, five,
and six-part chords. Repetitive and aimless melody is
merely result of chords. In D. (In 2.3, 1 p.) Fngr.
Biog. Ch.

3.114 WAXMAN, DONALD. Second Year Pageant.
Practical mix of traditional appeal and moderate con-

temporary traits. Consistent pianistic style. Composer's preface "To progress surely and musically,
with open ears ..." has been fulfilled. Music contains added-note and polychords, some modal writing,
and final cadences on tonic inversions or on the dominant as contemporary features. Keys through A and
B-flat. Allegretto Skip Dance has two-note slurs of
broken fifths and sixths, useful for rotary motion. LH
ostinato with RH creates dissonant sevenths and some
polyharmony. Bell Song, resonant with fourths and
fifths, is useful for pedal, LH thumb under, LH shifts
from treble to bass, and up to three-tone chords for
both hands. The Little Witch has lively forearm
strokes and RH moving over LH. Interior cadences
on dominant over tonic. Pleasant Water Music rolls
hand over hand with ascending and descending broken
chords, washed together by pedal. In the blend are
non-harmonic tones, some polyharmonies. Fine study
for even dynamics and note lengths. A of Allegro Indian Fires is in c dorian; B is in d dorian. LH has
repeated double notes, RH legato double notes. Sturdy
Finale will develop strength in both hands on legato
and staccato two and three-note chords. (The Mill
Wheel, p 12, p 16 and p 24.) (Galx, 1958, 26 pp.)
23 pieces. Fngr, some Ped. Ch. 3, some 2 & 4.

3.115 ZUPKO, RAMON. Cradle Song (1960).
Tender mood. RH has double notes with one tone
sometimes held. Deft pedal necessary for legato repeated tones in both melody and acc. In 6/4. In C
and E. (LR, 1962, 3 pp.) Fngr, MM.

3.116 ZUPKO, RAMON. Evening Song (1960).
Simple traditional melody harmonized with sensitivity.
Distinct tonal melody, with polyharmonic second inver-
sion acc. Meter shifts from 2/4 through to 5/4.
(LR, 1962, 2 pp.) Fngr, MM.

LEVEL 4

4. 1 American Composers of Today.
Excellent introduction to sweep of contemporary American music. Collection is economical source for browsing through music of thoroughly trained composers. Eighteen works are chosen for review. (See 3. 14, 3. 27, 3. 34, 3. 41, 4. 26, 4. 62, 4. 109, 4. 114, 4. 117, 4. 147, 5. 18, 5. 30, 5. 33, 5. 40, 5. 59, 5. 93, 5. 134 and 5. 144.) Preface informative. Contains music by Babbitt, Berger, Berkowitz, Castelnuovo-Tedesco, Cazden, Cowell, Dello Joio, V. Fine, Gideon, Harrison, Helps, Hovhaness, Meyerowitz, Mills, Overton, Prostakoff, Rathaus, Sessions, Slonimsky, Starer, Sydeman, and Weber. (Pp 3, 26, 30, 33, and 38.) (Mrk, 1965, 38 pp.) 23 pieces, 22 composers. Some Fngr, MM & Ped. Biog. 4 & 5, some 3.

4. 2 American Music by Distinguished Composers, Book 2, ed by Isadore Freed.
Like 3. 1, a splendid collection. Nine pieces reviewed. (See 4. 32, 4. 56, 4. 100, 4. 101, 4. 121, 4. 159, 5. 74, 5. 87 and 5. 109.) Contains music by Cowell, Gerschefski, Kraft, McBride, Moore, Pisk, Riegger, and Wagenaar. (Pr, 1966, 23 pp.) 10 pieces, 8 composers. Fngr, MM, Ped. *Anal. 4, some 5.

4. 3 Bulgarian Piano Music, Contemporary, Book 1, ed by Otto Daube.
Three numbers are contemporary; four are rather conservative, two are too conservative. Six are reviewed. (See 4. 71, 4. 103, 4. 116 and 5. 146.) All are well constructed. Contains music by Iliev, Nenov, Pipkov, Raitschev and Tepkov. Introduction and biographes in English and German, titles also in Bulgarian. (HG, 1965, 18 pp.) 9 pieces, 5 composers. Some Fngr, MM & Ped. *Biog. 4 & 5, some 6.

4.4   Canadian Festival Album, Vol. 2, ed by Rachel Ca-
       valho.
       Four works reviewed.   (See 3.26, 4.30, 4.31 and
       4.73.) Others too conservative.   Contains music by
       Coulthard, Fiala, Harmer, Jaque, Johnson, LaMarche
       and Street.   (BMI, 1966, 27 pp.) 12 pieces, 7 com-
       posers. Fngr, some MM & Ped. 4, some 3.

4.5   CLARK, FRANCES, compiler.   Contemporary Piano
          Literature, Book 5.
       (See 2.1.) Two of the six works first published after
       1950 felt worthy of review.   (See 4.47.) Three are
       too conservative.   Contains music by Bartók, Finney,
       Kabalevsky, Prokofiev and Tcherepnin.   (P 20.) (SB,
       1957, 35 pp.) 19 pieces, 5 composers.   Fngr, some
       MM, Ped. *Biog.

4.6   CLARK, FRANCES, compiler.   Contemporary Piano
          Literature, Book 6.
       (See 2.1.) Five of the six works first published after
       1950 are reviewed.   (See 4.46 and 4.155.) Contains
       music by Bartók, Finney, Kabalevsky, Prokofiev and
       Tcherepnin.   (SB, 1957, 41 pp.) 11 pieces, 5 com-
       posers. Fngr, some MM & Ped. *Biog. 4 & 5.

4.7   Czech and Slowak Piano Music, Contemporary, Book
          I, ed by Jan Matějček.
       Engaging works by composers born between 1882 and
       1928.   Moderate contemporary traits.   Seven pieces
       are reviewed.   (See 4.81, 4.104, 4.144, 5.91, 5.135
       and 5.150.) Two works in other collections.   (See
       4.144 and 5.135) Contains music by Kalabis, Kardoš,
       Krička, Martinů, Novák, Slavický, Sluka, Suchoň and
       Trojan.   Foreword, biographies and titles in English,
       German and Czech.   (HG, nd, 18 pp.) 10 pieces, 9
       composers.   Some Fngr, MM, Ped. *Biog. 4 & 5,
       some 6.

4.8   Hungarian Composers, Easy Piano Pieces By, ed by
          Károly Váczi.
       Outstanding volume presents attractive contemporary
       music, well planned for various pianistic explorations.
       Particularly useful for scale organizations other than
       major and minor.   Eight of the thirty-two pieces are
       fine but too conservative for description.   Twenty-four
       are reviewed.   (See 2.25, 2.47, 3.16, 3.103, 3.105,
       3.107, 4.34, 4.57, 4.67, 4.80, 4.86, 4.152, 4.153,

5.54 and 5.94.) Print, smaller than usual though
clear, allows more music on page. Contains music by
Borgulya, Daróczi, Decsényi, Geszler, Hajdu, Horusitzky, Járdányi, Kadosa, Kalmár, Kókai, Loránd,
Mező, Sugár, Szabó, Szelényi, Szervánszky, Szokolay
and Tardos. Preface and titles in Hungarian, English
and German. (EMB, 1961, 33 pp.) 32 pieces, 18
composers. Some Fngr & MM. Some Ch. 4, some
2, 3 & 5.

4.9   International Library of Piano Music, Album 8.
      Outstanding choice of composers and works. Covers
      Impressionist and Twentieth Century periods. Available
      only by purchasing entire set of nine albums. Six of
      the nine works first published after 1950 are reviewed.
      (See 3.11, 4.28, 4.68, 6.43 and 7.48.) Contains works
      by Badings, Bartók, Benson, Blacher, Casella, Copland,
      Cowell, Debussy, Dello Joio, Dohnányi, Falla, Fliar-
      kowsky, Fortner, Glière, Gretchaninoff, Hindemith,
      Hovhaness, Ives, Jelinek, Kabalevsky, Khatchaturian,
      Kodály, Krenek, Martin, Mennin, Miaskovsky, Milhaud,
      Mompou, Palmgren, Piston, Poldini and Prokofieff.
      (University Society, 268 pp.) 74 pieces, 32 composers.
      Some Fngr, MM, Ped. 4 & 6, some 3 & 5.

4.10 Magyar Szerzők Szontina Albuma, ed by Károly Váczi.
      Three works in this Sonatina Album by Hungarian Com-
      posers reviewed. (See 4.78, 5.66 and 5.145.) Some
      too conservative for this study. Contains music by
      Arányi, Decsényi, Hajdu, Járdányi, Kadosa, Sárai,
      Szelényi, Székely, Szokolay and Tardos. (Pp 7, 35,
      41, 55 and 65.) (EMB, 1963, 74 pp.) 10 pieces, 10
      composers. Fngr, some Ped. 4 & 5.

4.11 Royal Conservatory of Music Pianoforte Examination,
      Grade VII.
      Two works (by E. Rubbra and T. Kenins) qualify for
      review in this collection of music since Bach. (See
      4.125 and 5.68.) (Har, 1968, 46 pp.) 21 pieces, 19
      composers. Fngr, some MM & Ped. 4 & 5.

4.12 Yugoslavian Piano Music, Contemporary, Book 1, ed
      by Rudolf Lück.
      Lovely folk tunes apparently used in some of these at-
      tractive pieces. All works except one reviewed, most-
      ly conservative. (see 2.49, 4.25, 4.35, 4.75, 4.96,
      4.115, 5.75 and 5.81.) Editing unusually careful. In-

troduction and biographies in English and German;
titles add Yugoslavian. Contains music by Bjelinski,
Despić, Jez, Kunc, Lhota Kalinski, Matičić, Radić,
Slavenski and Tajčević. (HG, 1966, 20 pp.) 13 pieces,
9 composers. Some Fngr, MM & Ped. *Biog. 4,
some 2, 3 & 5.

4.13 ADORIAN, ANDREW. Pet's Corner.
Clever works sparkle with bright sounds and imagina-
tiveness. Pets like the "Budgeriger," for instance, certain to bring delight. Chromatic additions to traditional tonal harmonies. Useful for moderate keyboard exploration. Momentarily displaced harmonies give sharp-
ness to The Black Cat. RH forearm staccato broken
octaves. In treble range. Rapid Sausage Dog gets
harmonic zest in chromatic appoggiaturas, secondary
dominants, and repeated major seconds. RH has forearm staccato broken chords. Goldfish has Andante cellolike melody with RH broken fourth chord ostinato. In
E-flat. In the expressive Tortoise LH melody moves
frequently by fourths, and RH by legato harmonic major
thirds, some in whole tone scale. Many cadences to
the dominant, delaying tonic of c until end. (P 4.)
(Chap-L, 1962, 10 pp.) 9 pieces. Fngr, MM. Ch.

4.14 AGAY, DENIS. Three Recital Dances.
Bright Prokofieff quality, with facile in-and-out-of-key
harmonies characterize these pieces. Black key explorations (with some extensions) and forearm staccatos
used. For the "bright and happy" Parade Polka final
succession of chords of D-flat to G-flat to E to D to
V-I in B-flat suggests the harmonic range. A chromatic bass line helps to hold such freely associated
chords together. As with other works, Waltz Serenade's musicality is effortlessly apparent. Harmonies
in each measure usually tonic and dominant, but tone
omission or chord inversion gives some newness.
Hands have equal use. Last piece is a bolero. (Pr,
1956 & 1964, 9 pp.) Fngr, MM.

4.15 AITKEN, HUGH. Three Connected Pieces.
Thoroughly modern, convincing and genuinely expressive music, subtitled Thirds, Melody, and Fifths. Notation benefits are (a) beat represented by half note
(with that half note equalling dotted half in Melody) and
(b) rhythmically independent upper part and lower ostinato notated in different meters. Thirds can use arm

weight on each separated third. Melody, in vacillating
dorian and aeolian modes, has linear counterpoint. Legato stepwise Fifths occur in each hand. Good pedal
study. (Oxf, 1968, 4 pp.) Some Ped.

4.16 ANGERER, PAUL. Stimmungen (1955).
Moods are full of unpretentious interest. Show Hindemith influences, with voice-leading governing many progressions. Linear counterpoint. Forms are traditional and clear. Each accidental applies only to the following note. The Andante Exalted (I) uses many fourths
and fifths, particularly parallel fifths in acc. Often
wide spacing between hands. Allegro Carefree (II) is
well titled. Rhythms of varied slurring and metrical
changes. Texture shifts from linear counterpoint to
one where acc has harmonic seconds or fifths with
added second. Sad (IV) shifts easily between two-
voice imitative texture and homophony. Flexibly tonal.
Translations are Joyful (III) and Pensive (V). (Dob,
1956, 6 pp.) 5 pieces.

4.17 ARCHER, VIOLET. Theme and Variations.
Hindemith influences shown in fine serious piece: many
fourths and fifths, linear counterpoint, and strong modern tonality. Var II noticeably changes theme's rhythm.
Usually coupled writing, with varied spacing and octave
changes. Var III through V move far from theme.
Var IV is slow waltz. Var V begins like fughetta in
two voices. Theme is transposed up a fifth for final
Var VI, Largo maestoso with fuller setting. (Wat,
1964, 4 pp.) MM.

4.18 ARCHER, VIOLET. Three Miniatures.
Unity accomplished by obvious devices new in the twentieth century: for instance, Dreaming is based on harmonic and broken fifths, different for each hand, with
no other harmonic organization. Dark Mood depicted
in part by jabbing acc of minor seconds. Useful for
forearm staccatos. Determination achieves its character partly from repeated bass tones and partly from
insistent upward chromatic struggles. Rhythmically
alive, including syncopations. (Wat, 1965, 3 pp.)
MM. 4, some 3.

4.19 BARATI, GEORGE. Invention.
Modern in abstractness and lean texture. In two-part
dissonant counterpoint, with exchange of material be-

tween hands and much contrary motion. Excellent for
hand independence, including different dynamics in
each hand. Has forearm staccato on varied intervals
and finger staccato on measured trills. (Mer, 1958,
2 pp.) Fngr. *Anal.

4.20 BECK, MARTHA. Sassy Piece.
Well-named brilliant piece. Form is AABCA. In section A, while RH is very tonal, LH has three ostinato
major chords moving unconcernedly stepwise. B has
harmonic fourths or fifths in each hand, totalling sometimes quartal harmony. Useful for forearm staccato
strokes. (Leeds-NY, 1959, 3 pp.) MM, Ped.

4.21 BETTS, LORNE M. A Little March and Night Song.
Fascinating play between modality and tonality. Little
March is tuneful and direct with many fourths in acc.
Dynamics move from mp to ff and back to pp. Night
Song has varied note lengths, including notated short
trills. LH acc has legato thirds. (Leeds-C, 1963, 1
p & 1 p.) Some Fngr, MM.

4.22 BETTS, LORNE M. Tarantella and Chorale Prelude.
In Tarantella insistent forward motion reaches many
peaks. Changes to unnotated 3/4 meter from 6/8
meter at second peak. Opportunity for fast chromatic
scales in both hands in both directions. LH has parallel triads, RH some extensions. (Chorale Prelude too
conservative.) (Leeds-C, 1963, 2 pp & 1 p.) MM.

4.23 BETTS, LORNE M. Waltz and Slow Dance.
Gentle pitch exploration in this bitter-sweet music creates growing satisfaction. Tonal center of the chromatic Waltz is A, yet throughout, A-flat is important;
at end E-flat is included in tonic chord on A. Slow
Dance gives practice for LH playing without looking at
keyboard, and for both hands playing harmonic triads
together. Parallel motion seventh chords. Modal.
(Leeds-C, 1963, 2 pp & 1 p.) Some Fngr, MM, Ped.

4.24 BIBALO, ANTONIO. Fire Miniaturer (1966).
Four Miniatures show folk song and dance influences.
Tonal melodies have unexpected chromaticisms, harmonies have more such surprises. In foreword (in
Danish) composer indicates collection written in honor
of Bartok. Reverie (1) wavers back and forth between
major and minor third of tonic triads. The Allegretto

con spirito Study for the Left Hand (2) is marked
"easy, unconstrained." Nearly perpetual motion for
LH has much rapid work for first and second fingers.
Melody has varied articulations. Translations are
Lonesome Doll (3) and Little Finale (4). (WH, 1966,
8 pp.) 4 pieces. Fngr, MM, some Ped. Ch. 4,
some 5.

4.25 BJELINSKI, BRUNO. Song of the Little Emigrant,
        Alarm and Fog Creeps Up.
      Poignant treble melody of Song set with consistent
      falling broken thirds or fourths. Major mode, until
      final phrygian color. Alarm has pianistic flair in hand
      alternation and in RH rapid work. Momentary flat col-
      oring. Hand staccato. Inward mood of Fog Creeps
      Up expressed by two angular lines in bass. Remote
      tonality and numerous chromatic tones make it more
      contemporary than first two. (In 4.12, 1 p, 2 pp &
      1 p.) Fngr, some MM. *Biog. 4, 3 & 4.

4.26 CAZDEN, NORMAN. Game.
      Spontaneous interest comes in part from 3/8 and 3/4
      measures interpolated into basic 2/4 motion. Folk
      type dance tune in treble range. Pure mixolydian mode
      on G for first and last sections; less carefree middle
      section is in F and other momentary colors. (In 4.1,
      2 pp.) Fngr. Biog. Ch.

4.27 CHAGRIN, FRANCIS. Tussle.
      Allegro of consistent construction and useful pianisms.
      Title derived from struggle to fit a figure, heard from
      the first, into one meter. Changes between 2/2, 3/2,
      and 3/4. In addition to seventh chords involving le-
      gato thirds in each hand there is secundal and quartal
      harmony. (Ric-L, 1963, 2 pp.) 1 min, 10 sec.
      Fngr, MM.

4.28 COPLAND, AARON. Down a Country Lane.
      Serious piece, "gently flowing, in a pastoral mood."
      Unusually consonant, with much motion by thirds. Mel-
      ody repeated in settings of skillful variety. Interest-
      ing blend of polyphonic and homophonic textures. Prac-
      tice for RH weak-finger melody in chordal setting.
      Fine pedal study. Commissioned by Life Magazine.
      (B&H, 1962--also in 4.9, 2 pp.) MM, Ped.

4.29 CORTÉS, RAMIRO. Prelude (1956).
Piece will fascinate intelligent performer by constant
polyrhythms and rhythmic transformations often using
changing meters. Music truly communicates; Allegro
shows complex yet transparently clear workings of
composer's mind. Graceful melody subordinate to
rhythm. Texture effectively varied. "The tonality is
a much dissonanted D Major." (Pr, 1958, 2 pp.)
Fngr, MM. *Anal.

4.30 COULTHARD, JEAN. Daredevil.
Pleasant and effective Allegro scherzando. Uses familiar harmonic materials in slightly new way. Quite
chromatic. Many broken chord grace notes. Rotary
motion. (BMI, 1965--also in 4.4, 3 pp.) Some Fngr.

4.31 COULTHARD, JEAN. Noon Siesta.
Lovely Lento poco rubato, mostly in two voices, upper
leading. Has successive beats divided by two and
three. In g, melody having no accidentals. Conservative. (BMI, 1965--also in 4.4, 2 pp.) Fngr, Ped.

4.32 COWELL, HENRY. Sway Dance.
A consistent, "tender," and undemonstrative Andante
con moto. Excellent practice in close-range double
notes including tone-clusters in one hand, often alternating with a single tone in the legato support. Mixolydian and aeolian modes used. (Mer, 1958--also in
4.2, 2 pp.) *Anal.

4.33 COX, DAVID. Indian Ritual Dance.
Approachable Moderato, using only tones in far Eastern Indian mode--d e f g-sharp a b-flat c-sharp d.
Augmented seconds surprisingly unnoticed even with
scalelike melody. Music very unified, most often in
two voices, one leading. However, frequent changes
to coupled writing, and to melody with chordal acc.
(Ric-L, 1963, 2 pp.) 1 min, 40 sec. Fngr, MM,
Ped.

4.34 DECSÉNYI, JÁNOS. Dance.
Feeling of the ages about this basic little Allegretto.
In three or four voices, with treble melody and bass
line almost equally active. Two legato voices in RH
need careful fingering. Modal progressions. Conservative. (In 4.8, 1 p.) Fngr.

4.35 DESPIĆ, DEJAN. Fanfare, Waltz and Duo Pastorale,
     Op. 43a.
     Imaginative tonal works of real character. Fanfare
     is extrovert with variety of textures attained by imita-
     tive, near-polyharmonic entries of fourths, chordal
     declamations still stressing fourths, and coupled writ-
     ing. The "suave" Waltz sounds like a broken music
     box because of polyharmony. Duo Pastorale is smooth-
     ly skillful. Aeolian mode on c-sharp, and sometimes
     C-sharp. One of the two voices has pattern of four
     tones; chords sometimes added. Chordal at cadences.
     (In 4.12, 1 p, 1 p & 1 p.) Fngr, MM, some Ped.
     *Biog. 5, 4 & 4.

4.36 DOLIN, SAMUEL. Little Toccata.
     Vital abstract Allegro with useful technical features.
     In perpetual motion, with many repeated tones and
     broken intervals (usually RH) using hand staccato. In
     a, with free chromaticism. Much dynamic variety,
     some unpredictable, and many accents. Melody rhyth-
     mically disjointed. (BMI, 1961--also in Royal Con-
     servatory of Music Grade VIII Pianoforte Examination,
     published by Harris, 2 pp.) Fngr.

4.37 DONATO, ANTHONY. Rock Crusher.
     Lively piece, marked "briskly, with precision." Much
     syncopation in treble melody. Dorian mode on d, as
     well as major modes on F and C are some of centers
     touched. Both RH and LH forearm and hand staccato.
     (JF, 1960, 2 pp.)

4.38 DOUBRAVA, JAROSLAV. Maličkosti (1953).
     Collection of Little Things shows splendid consistency.
     2/8 and 3/16 meters, hence useful for thirty-second
     note introduction at this level of difficulty. Explores
     beats divided variously by four. Tonal, with free use
     of all twelve tones. Very few chords. Often treble
     range only. Day Dreaming (IV) has A-flat melody in
     LH. Acc only a broken seventh ending on dominant.
     Playfully and Wildly (V) does, indeed, provide fun.
     Against repeated A-flat chord, treble frolics between
     leading tone as temporary objective and as grace note
     to accented tonic. When that arrives, meter changes
     from 2/8 to 3/8. Perhaps many accents justify Wildly
     in title. Translations are Sadly (I), Mischievously (II),
     Longing (III). (Sup, 1954, 10 pp.) 5 pieces. Fngr,
     Ped. 4 & 5.

4.39 DZIELSKA, JADWIGA. Kolorowe Kamyki.
Colored Stones collection is spontaneously musical.
Highly recommended for free use of all twelve tones
in a tonal framework. For instance, A Dance (p 19)
has melody only in C, but opening acc of broken perfect fifths are on E-flat, F-sharp and B-flat. Kaleidoscope (p 17) modulates rapidly, moving from C to B,
D-flat, A, e, B-flat, D-flat, C, F and E, all in fifteen sparse measures. Predominantly homophonic textures, in two unequal parts, only two chords have as
many as four voices. Hands frequently above each
other. In Little Clouds, (p 13) LH on black keys is
above RH on white keys; later they get tangled.
Throughout collection legato is dependent on fingers,
no pedal necessary. Fine articulation variety. Optimistic nature of the pieces as well as some titles may
be most suitable for children, or young minded adults.
Art work is lovely. More music printed on a page
than usual. Translations are Snow is Falling and
Peony (p 4), Colored Stones (p 5), Swans (p 6), Two
Funny Men (p 7), After Rain (p 8), Trail in the Woods
(p 9), Bird (p 10), Dialogue (p 11), Moon (p 12), Steps
(p 14), Lily of the Valley (p 15), Flower Girl (p 16),
and Beautiful Ribbon (p 18). (PWM, 1961, 16 pp.) 17
pieces. Fngr. MM. 4 & 5, some 3.

4.40 ELWELL, HERBERT. Busy Day.
Well titled. Convincing and original. Uses three different modes, as well as major. In five sections,
fourth a development of first. Fourths are important
in third section. Unusual number of pianistic prac-
tices: coupled writing in sixths and tenths, staccato
fourths, and double notes alternating with held tone.
(Pr, 1957, 2 pp.) Fngr. *Anal.

4.41 ELWELL, HERBERT. Plaint.
Intense and satisfying. Fine rhythmic swing, as if
mourner were comforting himself by his own swaying.
Close-range four-part texture. Fine balance between
polyphony and homophony. RH needs singing tone with
weaker fingers. (Pr, 1957, 2 pp.) Fngr. *Anal.

4.42 ESCALANTE, EDUARDO. Suite No. 1 (1968).
Conservative, pleasant, and tasteful works in fluent
two-voice counterpoint. Very consistent. RH usually
most important, but LH is active; hands are independent. One work is in E, another in E-flat; one is in

mixolydian mode, another in aeolian. Very few accidentals. Three use only treble staff. Frequent habanera rhythms. Available translations are Song of the
Wheel (I), Lullaby (II), Little Tango (IV), and Embo-
lada (V) which latter are folklore arrangements, such
as improvised repartee between two balladeers. (IVi,
1968, 10 pp..) 5 pieces. Fngr, MM. 4 & 6, some
5.

4.43 ETHRIDGE, JEAN. Sunday Morning.
       Pleasantly poetic. Natural use of arm weight on
       chords because of octave shifts. In A-flat. Added-
       note chords and polyharmonies. Fine pedal study.
       (BMI, 1966, 2 pp.) Fngr, MM, Ped.

4.44 FIALA, GEORGE. Australian Suite, Op. 2.
       Clever and appealing works. "The seven parts ... are
       musical impressions of ... representatives of Austral-
       ian wild life," with information about each kind. Three
       slower pieces need emotional maturity; fast works are
       jolly and carefree. Consistent technical requirements.
       Chromaticisms lead to mild harmonic surprises. Con-
       servative. Black Swan, marked Tempo di Barcarola,
       has lovely RH melody. Broken chord acc extending to
       an eleventh may be played between hands or entirely by
       LH; pedal used. Adagio Koala fine study for RH tone.
       Harmony is individual: while acc is often alternating
       legato harmonic fourths third apart and centered on ton-
       ic, melody hovers on and around leading tone. (Also
       in 3.2.) Allegretto giocoso (indeed playful) Kookaburra
       has splendid usefulness for hand staccato playing. Ar-
       ticulation challenging. (BMI, 1963, 14 pp.) 7 pieces.
       MM. Ch. 4, some 3.

4.45 FIALA, GEORGE. Sonatina, Op. 1.
       Very sensitive music. Admirable handling of contem-
       porary harmony. Serious Andantino melancolico has
       subtle coloring from chromaticisms. In aeolian mode
       on a. Some fourth chords. Gracefully curved melody.
       Larghetto expressivo in dorian mode on c-sharp, with
       parallel fourths dominating harmony. Allegro leggiero
       Tarantella has strength from pedals of harmonic fifths,
       and from melodic fourths and fifths. Former often
       half tone "off" in polymodal or modal/tonal harmony.
       Ends marcato with bass octave strides. (BMI, 1960,
       8 pp.) 3 movements. MM. 4 & 5.

4.46 FINNEY, ROSS LEE. Hopping, Swinging, Night and
     Running Around (1957).
     Hopping is "lively." Twelve-tone work described in
     comments. Usually in two imitative voices of varied
     slurring; also three-tone chords spanning major sev-
     enth. Order of twelve-tone set in Swinging includes
     common triads which overlap, and polyharmony re-
     sults. As tension mounts, added-note chords enter.
     In 2/2, played "not too fast." Fine study in dynam-
     ics. Night is sensitive twelve-tone music. Much use
     of retrograde transformation of set. In two voices of
     wide intervals. Perpetual motion ostinato-like acc
     uses intervals from two common triads. Thumb-under
     practice. Equal hand emphasis. (In 4.6, 1 p, 1/2 p,
     1-1/2 pp, 2 pp.) Fngr, some MM. *Anal, *Biog.
     4, 4, 5 & 5.

4.47 FINNEY, ROSS LEE. Song and Vacation (1957).
     Song has lovely sound, with sostenuto pedal for fuller
     texture. Melody uses only four tones with octave shifts.
     "In a swinging tempo" ostinato is legato thirds and
     sixth of one chord, wavering between major and minor.
     Equal hand emphasis. Vacation moves fluently and
     "gayly." In lydian mode on A. Rapid melody usually
     in five-finger position. Acc is slower, with forearm
     staccato triads moving by step. (In 4.5, 1 p & 1 p.)
     Fngr, some Ped. *Biog.

4.48 FLOYD, CARLISLE. Episodes, Vol. 1.
     Fluent melodies of mildly original profile. Useful for
     developing lyricism with legato fingering and little ped-
     al. Pianistically consistent. Using no signatures,
     keys mostly of few sharps and flats, but modulations
     may range widely. Free use of all twelve tones.
     Some are modal. Rhythmically conservative. Divided
     between works in two-voice texture and works with
     melody and acc. Page turns may be inconvenient.
     Fourth Lyric Piece (Allegro moderato) is slightly ex-
     ploratory, wandering among flats and sharps. LH has
     legato chords in two-beat grouping. An Ancient Air in
     Overtone scale, always pp with drone acc. Pedal indi-
     cations blur several measures. RH melody of Lullaby
     has lovely angular line. Lydian mode on G, E & C.
     Acc always tonic and submediant chords in first inver-
     sion. Four-voice chords in Chorale played sharply
     staccato. Modulations quite ingenious, dissonance
     noticeable. Wind Song in 5/8--three plus two and re-

versed. Splendid keyboard exploration with mild extensions. Burletta delightful Allegro vivace. While RH
melody soars up and down with varied intervals LH has
intermittent added-note chord punctuations. (B&H, 1965,
13 pp.) 13 pieces. Fngr, MM. 4, some 3 & 5.

4.49 FRANCHETTI, ARNOLD. Chant.
Fascinating in its use of parallel triads, related to be-
ginnings of harmony. Tenor melody, played often by
LH thumb, harmonized by three-tone chords. Chords
are non-legato, or of irregular slurred lengths. Much
lydian mode. B-flat and F-sharp are only accidentals.
(Pr, 1958, 2 pp.) Fngr, MM. *Anal.

4.50 FRANCO, JOHAN. Toccata.
Extrovert. One melody line only. "An excellent
'touch' piece emphasizing control of detached notes in
alternate hands." Hands alternate irregularly. Dynamic variety. Pure D. Conservative. (Dit, 1952, 2 pp.)
Fngr, MM.

4.51 FREED, ISADORE. Sonatina No. 1.
Directions "gay" and "spirited" indicate attractiveness.
Agile melodies, neo-classic temperament, and tonality
using all twelve tones are handled with skill. Suggests
music of Hindemith. Main melody usually in treble.
RH legato finger emphasis in first movement; LH acc
often double notes. Form of slow second movement
broadly indicated by tonic pedal in first section and
dominant pedal in middle section. Repeated melodies
varied. Rondo is unified by repeated-tone motive.
Smooth brief modulations. (SMP, 1954, 5 pp.) 3
movements. MM. 4 & 5.

4.52 FÜSSL, KARL HEINZ. 5 Tones--5 Fingers (1941-1959).
Exquisitely crafted works of moderate originality and
impressive logic. Five-finger positions with no thumb
under allow for shifts within a piece and unusual patterns, different for each hand. Two of three slower
pieces may seem too abstract on first acquaintance.
Solemn 1, using forearm staccatos, is two-voice canon
at augmented or major sixth. Notable rhythmic drive
in Vivo 3. LH acc always sforzando on thumb covering
two tones. RH melody secondary to rhythm, uses only
G A C D E or A C D E G. Often one-line, 6 is played
"freely," "like a cadenza." LH has first five tones of
e, RH first five tones of C lydian mode. (UE 13679,

1966, 9 pp.)   6 pieces.   6 min, 30 sec.   MM.

4. 53 GARCIN, MICHEL.   The Clown.
Accessible.   This very expressive clown has poignancy
from mild clash of seconds and dissonant contrary motion.   Bass chromatic line gives direction.   Medium
wide range.   Many two-note slurs.   (In 3. 6, 2 pp.)
Some Fngr, MM.   Ch.

4. 54 GASULEAS, STEPHANOS.   11 Aphorismen.
Aphorisms are indeed terse,   longest being twenty-one
measures, but often poetic with graceful line.   Mostly
one-line music of moderately wide range.   Same
twelve-tone tone set, frequently transposed, used for
all selections.   Segment of first four tones appears often as harmonic minor third and perfect fourth.   Numerous meter changes and rests.   Foreword, in German and English, by Jelinek.   (UE 13182, 1961, 5
pp.)   4 & 5.

4. 55 GEORGE, EARL.   Lento (1963).
Lovely neo-romantic music.   Many broken eleventh and
thirteenth chords, sometimes not resolved.   Three
tones of LH extended broken chords may cover double
octave plus fifth.   RH includes double notes, mostly
thirds, sixths or sevenths.   (Oxf, 1967, 2 pp.)   MM,
Ped.

4. 56 GERSCHEFSKI, EDWIN.   Song of the Mountains.
Appealingly lyrical.   Uses RH weak fingers for singing
touch with double notes.   Typical melody/acc texture;
latter uses extended broken triads.   Fine pedal study.
Conservative.   (Mer, 1957--also in 4. 2, 3 pp.)   Fngr,
MM, Ped.   *Anal.

4. 57 GESZLER, GYÖRGY.   Etude.
Haunting piece is most consistent Andantino con moto
fragment.   LH climbs and descends only tones of b
harmonic minor scale with thirds and a tonic pedal,
while RH murmurs in shorter stepwise tones of repeated patterns.   LH in 3/4, RH 6/8.   Splendid for
dynamic evenness and control.   Conservative.   (In 4. 8,
1/2 p.)   Fngr.

4. 58 GOEB, ROGER.   Jesting.
"This sprightly music with its percussive bite is actu-
ally in a disguised form of G major."   Each hand

ranges widely with hand and forearm staccatos.   Many
mischievous minor seconds.   Much unity from first
rhythmic motive, and from other repetitions.   Many
"silent beats."   (Mer, 1957, 2 pp.)   Fngr, MM.
*Anal.

4.59 GORDON, LOUIS.   Junior Jazz.
Foreword states: "These short pieces ... give a
cross section of some of the many styles and techniques of Jazz which can be played by students at any
stage of development.   They are sophisticated, yet
simple and imaginative."   Rhythms sometimes tricky.
Slow and expresive Cloudy Night has many added-note
chords.   West Coasty indeed has "interesting harmonies;" for instance, F tonic chord is not heard until final measures.   Harmonies, often secondary dominants, move in parallel motion.   Accents often antici-
pate the beat.   Fast Riffs has two rhythmic patterns:
first has silence at halfway point of first beat; second
has each last half beat accented in RH.   In Jumpin'
Jacks dotted rhythms of 1920's and unexpected accents
are combined.   Parallel chromatic harmonies.   (Mrk,
1961, 11 pp.)   9 pieces.   Fngr, some Ped.   *Anal.
4, some 3.

4.60 GOULD, MORTON.   Abby Variations.
Attractive and inventive, making much from little.
Tones of a b b e (e for y) used for theme.   Concerning the twelve variations: two has staccato descending
triads in the bass; three is neo-romantic, with parallel broken seventh chords; five is "stately, bell-like;"
six uses staccato ostinato ranging an eleventh in its
more difficult version; eleven is neo-classic and twelve
has imitation.   "Happy Birthday to You" woven into
ending.   Much pianistic variety throughout, and few
troublesome modernisms.   (G&C, 1964, 9 pp.)   Some
Ped.   Ch.

4.61 GUARNIERI, M. CAMARGO.   Acalanto (1954).
Lullaby is a sensitive "calm and ingenuous" number,
essentially simple but with amazing variety.   Lyrical
RH melody has grace notes covering as much as a
tenth.   Acc of broken intervals (many fourths), while
centered on a, has much chromaticism.   Ending indicates aeolian mode on e.   Treble range only.   (Ric-
BA, 1957, 2 pp.)   Some Fngr, MM.

4.62 HARRISON, LOU. Little Suite for Piano.
Expressive work economical, yet remarkably varied
within five-finger position for each hand. Meter is unbarred but effect is clear; bar's omission may help
clarify cross rhythms and onward flow. Pastorale,
lilting, homophonic, alternates role of hands. Homespun spontaneity rules in Quadrille, emphasizing broken
triads in each hand. LH is fast Alberti-like ostinato.
Much mirror motion in Chorale. (In 4.1, 3 pp.) 3
movements. Biog.

4.63 HARVEY, PATRICK. Music for Two Dancers.
"Calm and Grave," dignified. Two dancers portrayed
by chordal bitonal material (mainly G and F), or melody and acc. Some inner voice emphasis with chords.
Fine pedal and tone study. (Ric-L, 1964, 2 pp.) 1
min, 50 sec. MM, Ped.

4.64 HAUBIEL, CHARLES. Gently.
Lovely sounds in this "Study in Sevenths." Sevenths
heard both as harmonic double notes and broken chords;
seconds which resolve also used. Practice for (a) RH
fifth finger mp and thumb pp on sevenths, (b) similar
separate dynamics in LH seconds, and (c) LH widely
spaced broken chords. Good pedal study. (JF 9426,
1962, 2 pp.) Fngr, MM, Ped.

4.65 HAUFRECHT, HERBERT. Song of the Valley.
Sentimental and loving. Long pedals blend moderately
wide ranges. LH crosses RH. Solidly in D, with a
few telling color changes. Conservative. (Mer, 1958
--also in 3.1, 2 pp.) Fngr, MM, Ped. *Anal.

4.66 HEMMER, EUGENE. American Miniatures.
Delightfully spontaneous. Evoke early rural America
in sparce and purposely awkward writing. Tonal harmonies appropriately crude. Foreword and biography
by Pia Gilbert. Frontier Valley, marked Adagio
maestoso, is theme with three variations and coda.
Usually in polyphonic texture, although one voice leads.
Thirds omitted from triads, dissonances unprepared
and unresolved. Meters of Mississippi Shuffle alternate
between 7/8 and 3/4. In F-sharp mixolydian with
chromatic inflections; tonic chord isn't found until final
cadence. Loping canter attractively captured by traditional rhythms in Cowboy's Holiday. In E, with prominent blues scale vagaries. (Orc, 1960, 9 pp.) 6 pieces.

4.67 HORUSITZKY, ZOLTÁN. Great Joy and Autumnal
      Leaves.
      In "resolute" Allegro Great Joy homespun quality
      comes from use of pentatonic mode, simple reiterated
      bass, and fourths in melody. Develops finger strength
      in both hands. Autumnal Leaves a lovely Andantino of
      consistency and technical usefulness. Has successive
      beats divided by three and two. LH near-ostinato has
      some fairly rapid skips. Melody in dorian mode on
      c, while acc has raised fourth. (In 4.8, 1 p & 1 p.)
      Fngr.

4.68 HOVHANESS, ALAN. Mountain Idylls.
      Both purity and exotic interest in these pieces. Moon
      Dance uses pure d dorian mode. Phrases always four
      measures long. LH acc uses only parallel broken tri-
      ads. RH melody of Mountain Lullaby (also in 4.9) pro-
      vides exotic interest through augmented seconds and
      short-long rhythms. Acc has two and three-tone clus-
      ter chords, good practice for playing without looking
      at keyboard. (AMP, 1955, 4 pp.) 3 pieces. MM,
      Ped.

4.69 HOVHANESS, ALAN. Sonatina, Op. 120.
      Near-Eastern mood most consistent. Little resem-
      blance to traditional sonatina. Synthetic mode with on-
      ly tones e f a b-flat b d and d-sharp used. First and
      last movements have melancholy melody in baritone
      register, accompanied by pp arpeggiated chords above
      and below. Middle movement often based on four-note
      LH ostinato from first movement. Faster note melody
      in high treble register. (Pet 6529, 1964, 7 pp.) 6
      min. MM.

4.70 HOVHANESS, ALAN. Three Haikus, Op. 113.
      Exotic atmosphere the title promises achieved by re-
      peated formulas and small-interval melodies, blended
      by long damper pedals. Eight-tone modes used in first
      and last number. I, an Adagio, has acc of broken
      major and minor sevenths. II, after harplike introduc-
      tion with polyrhythm of nine against five, has melody
      in high register accompanied by repeating alternate
      lower tones. In the Adagio III an unmeasured baritone-
      register melody (with prominent augmented seconds)
      alternates with slightly changing, lower register chord
      clusters. (Pet 66028, 1968, 5 pp.) 3 min. MM. 4
      & 5.

4.71 ILIEV, KONSTANTIN.   The Hen Laid an Egg and The
       Cuckoo.
       Hen's happy clucking heard in rapid repeated tones.
       Fast mixolydian tune accompanied by Alberti bass and
       cluster chords which gradually accumulate tones.
       Lovely Cuckoo begins and ends with traditional minor
       third, noticeable here for cross relation.   Main melody
       in aeolian mode on b-flat is expressively accompanied
       by parallel sixths or fifths.   (In 4.3, 2 pp & 1 p.)
       Some Fngr. *Biog.   5 & 4.

4.72 JAQUE, RHENÉ.   Dance.
       Gay, extrovert musicality.   Diatonic, with some chro-
       maticism; whole-tone scale suggested.   Parallel har-
       monic fourths, and fourth chords.   Varied dynamics.
       Traditional rhythm.   (BMI, 1962, 2 pp.)   MM.

4.73 JAQUE, RHENÉ.   Jesting.
       Graceful and fluent RH melody using scales.   Each
       hand has small extensions.   Phrygian mode.   Color
       contrast in middle section.   (BMI, 1962--also in 4.4
       with Fngr, 2 pp.)   MM.

4.74 JAQUE, RHENÉ.   Rustic Dance.
       Spontaneous and attractive neo-classic music.   Variety
       between d dorian and major modes.   Harmonic fourths
       and fifths in parallel motion.   (BMI, 1962--also in 3.2,
       2 pp.)   MM.

4.75 JEŽ, JAKOB.   The Little Boat is Departing.
       Lovely melody in Andante cantabile tempo.   A pastel
       in b with mild chromatic coloring.   LH acc has broken
       chords.   Conservative.   (In 4.12, 1 p.)   Fngr, MM.
       *Biog.

4.76 JOLIVET, ANDRÉ.   Chansons Naïves (1951).
       Beautiful Naive Songs, Six Children's Pieces for Piano,
       are splendid works.   Aptly titled, but require talent to
       play them; they are not simple, either in technique or
       interpretation.   If titles like Song for a Breton Doll
       (p 5) are acceptable, performer could be older.   Famil-
       iar modal and harmonic materials used with originality.
       Some lovely small-range melodies are like folk songs.
       Textures basically homophonic; require little pedal.
       Traditional rhythms.   Octave reach.   Watching the
       Flies Fly (p 2) has graceful melody with prominent
       leaps; LH acc of same general character.   Sounds of

the Carillon (p 8) evoked by embedding melody in double
notes ranging from thirds through sevenths, by acc resembling ostinato, and by long damper pedals. Dance
of the Little Sioux (p 10) is no ordinary Indian Dance,
except for the usual roughness. Treble melody generally moves by small steps, while single line bass leaps
awkwardly. In dorian mode, first on e-flat, then
brightens to g and b, turns back to e-flat and ends on
b-flat. (Noël, 1951, 10 pp.) 6 pieces. MM, some
Ped. Ch. 4 & 5.

4.77 JOLIVET, ANDRÉ. Lullaby in a Hammock.
      Tasteful lyric number, in undemonstrative French man-
      ner. Splendid opportunity for developing singing treble
      line. LH acc has somewhat extended, mildly explora-
      tory double notes, with lower or upper note moving
      twice as fast. Deft pedaling needed for purely legato,
      lovely music. (In 3.6, 2 pp.) Fngr.

4.78 KADOSA, PÁL. Sonatine.
      Sprightly with varied articulations. Concentrated the-
      matic material almost tuneful. Slight chromatic ex-
      plorations are the only modernisms. Poco allegro
      tempo. Much forearm staccato. Second theme derives
      rhythmic interest from rests on main beats. Develop-
      ment uses only first theme. Much small-step motion,
      minor sixth the largest harmonic interval. Conserva-
      tive. (In 4.10, 3 pp.) 1 movement. Fngr. MM.

4.79 KADOSA, PÁL. Three Small Pieces.
      Solid content and fine harmonic interest, with quartal
      harmony emphasized. Use rotary forearm motion.
      Title also in Hungarian and German. One has extro-
      vert Allegro play on polyharmonic passages in fourths
      and slower strong forearm jabs. Two is expressive
      Andante with improvisatory harmonies. Three, marked
      Giocoso, is lively with variety in dynamics and articu-
      lation. Contrary motion with slurred fourths or scales.
      Unexpectedly ends in F-sharp. (EMB, 1965, 6 pp.)

4.80 KADOSA, PAL. Three Small Piano Pieces on Bach's
      Name.
      Each begins with "Bach" motto--B-flat A C B. First
      is spontaneous, witty Tempo guisto, with shifts between
      2/2, 1/2 and 3/4. Fluent chromatic treble melody.
      The Poco andante usually has two moderately chromatic
      lines. Well-named Presto scherzo diabolico uses ac-

cented RH octaves (LH broken octaves) as well as
polytonal broken chords in both hands. (In 4. 8, 2-1/2
pp.) Fngr.

4. 81 KALABIS, VIKTOR. About a Fountain.
Moderato, cantabile has lovely melody centered in b
aeolian mode, straying greatly in middle section. Entirely coupled writing in sixths. Expressive cross relations. (In 4. 7, 1 p.) Fngr, MM, Ped. *Biog.

4. 82 KANN, HANS. Sonatine (1954).
Homespun, refreshingly original. Sentiment present,
but not for long. Sensitive to aural effect of different
spacings in homophonic texture. Tonal, although adventurous in a transparent way. Uses symbol of H‾
to point out main melody. Traditional rhythm. Planning necessary for legato playing. Long Allegro leggiero beginning is typical of Austrian sweetness; soon
there are telling dissonances, such as successive or
simultaneous cross relations. In second movement,
marked "expressive," melodic fragment is ingeniously
repeated: increasingly fuller textures, changed spacings and dynamics added. Andante leggiero has simple
humor, with repetition of bass seventh chords and
treble staccato patter. Rondo is delightfully naive ending. (Dob, 1961, 7 pp.) 4 movements. Some Ped.
4 & 5.

4. 83 KARKOFF, MAURICE. Oriental Pictures, Op. 66.
Serious music of distinct character. Exotic harmonies
usually broadly tonal but resist categorizing. Splendid
rhythmic variety with Oriental influences. Melodies
usually move by small steps. First works clearly programmatic; later ones more abstract. Titles also in
Swedish. Undemonstrative Lamentation unified with
short-range melody and double note acc. Usually lower
tone of acc is anchored while upper tone moves chromatically. Good study in dynamics. Camel Ride uses
an often accented and suddenly shorter note melody
with staccato ostinato acc. The brooding Tending to
Darkness gives rhythmic practice for varied but short
note patterns. Narrow melodic range. In Front of the
Walls of Jerusalem is an Andante sostenuto in recita-
tive rhythms, triplets, and a frequently tied note.
Wider keyboard range than usual; harmonies, following
little system, are more dissonant. (Geh, 1966, 11
pp.) 8 pieces. MM, Ped. 4 & 5.

4. 84 KASEMETS, UDO. Prelude, Op. 30, No. 2 (1952).
Lively. In words of composer, a meditation "... on
twelve-note serial, rhythmical, and metrical questions." Twelve-tone basis doesn't preclude pattern
repetitions like tonic and dominant in C. Beyond notated 3/8 meter, there are two-beat patterns, as well
as other polyrhythms. Hands often quite far apart.
(In 8. 1, 2 pp.) MM. Biog.

4. 85 KASZYCKI, LUCJAN M. Children's Variations (1952).
Childlike and delightful. Title loosely used, family
resemblances between attractive melodies very general.
Usually RH melody, LH acc, with both hands in treble
range. Each work definitely in C with unusual amount
of decorative chromaticism at this level of difficulty.
A few octave reaches. Traditional forms and rhythms.
Titles also in Polish. In the Train, first part accelerates and last part slows. Each hand non-legato, often with broken chords. Lullaby acc uses LH extensions. In staccato Polka, RH melody, often quickly
crossing LH, is usually in different five-finger positions. LH fifth finger darts back and forth among
chord tones. (PWM, 1954, 9 pp.) 6 pieces. Fngr,
some Ped. Ch.

4. 86 KÓKAI, REZSÖ. Rhapsody.
Gives splendid opportunity for authoritative interpreta-
tion in a freely declamatory manner, unusual at this
level of difficulty. Resolute passages in coupled texture and dotted rhythm alternate with expressive parlando rhythm. Tonal, with free use of chromatic
tones. (In 4. 8, 1-1/2 pp.) Fngr, MM.

4. 87 KUBIK, GAIL. Quiet Time (1957).
Thoughtful. Felicitous details, like momentary secondary voices. Gracefully curved melody and supporting
harmonies sometimes make dissonances of gentle coloring. Uses singing tone and some octaves. (Pr, 1959,
3 pp.) Fngr. *Anal.

4. 88 KURKA, ROBERT. Sonatina for Young Persons.
Appealing. Fast movements glory in energy expendi-
ture. Spontaneous jazz idiom. Tonal. Combines
Theme and two Variations with two interpolated, unrelated, slower Canzonettas. Equal hand emphasis.
Opening Vivo Theme emphasizes broken chords and
syncopated melody. Harmonic seconds add zest to acc.

Needs strong fingers. Prestissimo Variation I has
many broken chords, as well as many sevenths and
seconds for harmonic material. Allegro Variation II
follows Theme very closely, varying it usually by halv-
ing note values. Such kaleidoscoping gives effective
conclusion. (Weint, 1966, 11 pp.) 5 movements. 4
& 5.

4.89 KURKA, ROBERT. Spring Planting and Sparkling
       Water.
Wonderfully happy music. First is in D, with arrest-
ing harmonic adventures. Sparkling Water uses repeated tones alternating between hands. In C, with
numerous modulations. Treble range only. (Weint,
1954 & 1960, 1 p & 1 p.) MM. Ch.

4.90 LANDOWSKI, MARCEL. En Trottinant sur le Sentier.
Stepping Lightly Along the Path is pleasant Allegretto.
Harmony has some originality: section A is polytonal;
B has an unrelated upper pedal and whole ends on
what is apparently a minor dominant chord. LH hand
staccato broken thirds and fifths, and RH repeated
tones. (HL, 1959, 2 pp.) Fngr.

4.91 LAWNER, MARK. Waltz.
Sensitive. Searching chromatic harmonies--maybe
too aimless. Graceful treble melody uses singing
touch. Too narrowly labeled as child's piece. (Weint,
1950, 2 pp.) Fngr.

4.92 LEIGHTON, KENNETH. Pieces for Angela, Op. 47.
Tuneful, and should be enchanting to youngsters. Both
successive and simultaneous cross relation much used.
Neoclassic. Phrases often four measures long. Pieces
alternate between fast and slow. The Clockwork Doll
humorously confined by mechanics: which inflection of
a tone will it be, and why be restricted to melodic
thirds and harmonic fifths? One hand often above or
below the other. Melody and acc alternate between
hands in Cradle Song. Acc splendid for wrist practice
with legato harmonic fifths, thirds, and seconds. Exquisite coloring in A Sad Folk Song from tones raised
when ascending, and lowered when descending; also,
from simultaneous cross relations. Fine for tone and
for short crescendos and decrescendos. Delightful
Leap Frog portrayed by vaulting syncopated melody and
acc of two quick slurs against the meter and outlining

a seventh. Texture changes to coupled writing. (Nov,
1967, 16 pp.) 8 pieces. Ch.

4.93 MacDONALD, MALCOLM. Entry of the Zanies.
Mock seriousness gleefully expresses title. Many
added-note staccato chords, some rapid because of
dotted rhythm. Starts in G and travels as far as e-
flat. Phrases often sequential. (Ric-L, 1960, 3 pp.)
MM.

4.94 MACONCHY, ELIZABETH. Mill Race.
A unique, merry perpetual motion Allegro ritmico.
Fine quality of inevitability. Alternates between 3/4
and 3/8; also has tussling between major and minor,
as well as some phrygian coloring. Added-note simple
chords. Fine dynamic variety. (Ric-L, 1963, 3 pp.)
1 min, 25 sec. Fngr, MM.

4.95 MAINVILLE, DENISE. Sonatine.
Fine combination of innocence and mild sophistication.
In F. At end, main theme turns towards whole tone
scale; this gradually leads toward second fragmentary
idea in cross rhythm mirror writing with some chromaticism. LH acc has broken fourths. No tempo indication. Measure fifteen needs an f-sharp in bass;
measure eighteen should have a g-natural at end;
measure thirty-six and thirty-seven should have b-flats
in treble. (AME, 1965, 2 pp.)

4.96 MATIČIĆ, JANEZ. Pavane.
Piquant color comes from bitonality (key signatures of
e and B-flat) and chromaticism. Acc offbeat chromatic
harmonic intervals or staccato broken chords. Mor-
dants give antique quality. (In 4.12, 1 p.) Fngr.
*Biog.

4.97 MELLERS, WILFRID. Cat Charms.
Refreshing, somewhat original, requiring sensitivity.
Dynamics usually soft. Composer groups works by
threes: for morning, afternoon, and night. He suggests instruments for improvised percussion to accompany miming of pieces. In For Hunting to irregular
rhythms result from varied articulations. LH acc has
irregularly placed simple added-note chords. In D,
sometimes with raised fourth and lowered seventh. For
Weaving to has finger staccato with lovely sounds from
pedal blends. Mostly black key pentatonic mode. For

Dancing to in Sunlight resembles vigorous old English
dance, with dotted rhythms in 6/8. Similar to dorian
mode, but with raised fourth. Texture either coupled
writing, sometimes three octaves apart, or drone bass
and melody. For Keeping Still in the Dark to creates
mood with high parallel fourths, sixths, and sevenths
interspersed with seconds, while LH repeats single low
tone. (Nov, 1965, 11 pp.) 9 pieces. Some Ped. Ch.

4.98 MILHAUD, DARIUS. Accueil Amical (1943-1945, 1947-
1948)
Friendly Welcome collection is sweetly naive. Splendid childlike moods. Lovely melodies. Many uncommon and ingenious details. Six works have no editing,
giving performer creative scope. In general, reaches
are not large, although there are some broken octaves;
in any case, much pedal is needed. Some pieces have
fragments that may cause sudden technical snags. One
line of melody is usually the only RH tones. Acc may
be a counter melody, but in more than half the numbers acc has double or, rarely, triple notes. Tonal
harmonies have freshness. Five works are ABA (da
capo) in form. Always tonal (no key signature), but
harmonic motion by step is frequent. Moderate range
only. Red Pajamas (p 1) acc has parallel second and
first inversion chords as well as parallel thirds.
Simple melody (often repetition of two tones) in Mary
Sleeps (p 6) harmonized by wandering dominant seventh
to tonic progressions, as well as by chromatic thirds.
The New Tooth (p 7) jauntily mixes sixteenths and triplets. Mademoiselle No. 5, in 5/4, is almost purely
in E-flat. Opening measure of melody becomes closing
repeated bass acc. Fast and always evolving Sweets
for August 16, 1948 Christening (p 16) has rapid passage work in exploratory black-white key relationships.
Solemn Letter from the Castle (p 17) is a chordal
study. Middle section has seventh chords exclusively
arranged as fifths in each hand. Translations are
Good Morning Violaine (p 2), Blue Pajamas (p 3),
Good Morning Dominic (p 4), Elma is Playing (p 5),
Good Morning Philipinna and "very fast, please" (p 9),
Peter Writes Commentaries (p 10), Marion is Painting
(p 11), Recreation and "without haste" (p 12), Kind
Hospitality, Dear Friends (p 13), Blind Man's Buff and
"as fast as possible" (p 14) and Little Peter Arrived
on a Beautiful Summer Day (p 15). (Heu, 1953, 17
pp.) 17 pieces. Ch. 4, some 2, 3 & 5.

4.99 MILHAUD, DARIUS. Play.
This graceful "without haste" music is in "movement
of a waltz." Sound pedagogical purposes. Mostly two-
part legato music moves smoothly from mixolydian and
lydian modes on C to brief passages in E-flat and G-
sharp. Sometimes coupled writing. (In 3.6, 1 p.)
Fngr.

4.100 MOORE, DOUGLAS. Dance for a Holiday.
Thoroughly enjoyable, with no contemporary problems.
Cultivates equal hand independence in melody/acc tex-
ture. Excellent for forearm staccatos. In aeolian
mode on f. (Pr, 1958--also in 4.2, 2 pp.) Fngr.
*Anal.

4.101 MOORE, DOUGLAS. Prelude.
Has convincing naturalness. Flowing legato needs sustained emotional concentration. Linear two-part texture, each hand pursuing interesting material. Many
melodic fourths, some mild extensions. Syncopation
in upper part. (Pr, 1958--also in 4.2, 2 pp.) Fngr.
*Anal.

4.102 MUCZYNSKI, ROBERT. Fables.
Graceful melodies almost tuneful. Frequently in two
voices, one always primary. Often modal. Even
though five works end with dissonances of added seconds, fourths and the like, dissonance level is not
high, except in two numbers. Seven pieces are Moderato or faster in tempo. Rhythms usually conservative. Melodies often move by step or along chord outline. Only one octave in entire collection. Four
marked without pedal. Piano writing is traditional. 3
begins and ends in C; middle section in mixolydian
mode on E-flat. Always in treble range. Four-part
harmony in Adagio 5, unusual for collection. Many
simultaneous cross relations and expressive appoggiaturas. 6 a non-legato Presto in lydian mode on F and
dorian mode on d and e-flat. LH acc highly unified.
8 has lyrical and very tonal melody; however, decorated dominant pedal is prominent and mixolydian harmonization used in middle section. (GS, 1967, 9 pp.)
9 pieces. Fngr, MM, Ped. 4, some 5.

4.103 NENOV, DIMITER. Pastorale and Musette.
Neo-romantic in temperament with medium full texture. Serious Pastorale requires concentration to sus-

tain interest in slow and few-note measures. In aeolian mode on d, with many whole-step cadences; some
lovely mildly chromatic chords. Short-long rhythms.
Middle section, marked "dreamily," is in 5/4 and
uses three-note ground bass. Musette is study in RH
weak-finger melody accompanied by notated trill with
first and second fingers. LH uses four-note wide-
range ostinato. Conservative. (In 4.3, 2 pp & 3 pp.)
Some Fngr & MM & Ped. *Biog. 4 & 6.

4.104 NOVÁK, JAN. Allegretto.
Amusing. Rhythm is tricky because in the perpetual
motion there are unnotated meter changes and constant
but irregular hand alternation. Melody reaches out,
both upward and downward, in an interesting manner.
Staccato and treble range only. Many gradual dynamic
changes. (In 4.7, 1 p.) *Biog.

4.105 OKUNJEV, G. Mabyenkich Dvenadtsat Pyes.
Twelve Little Pieces show much imagination, with titles
often aptly portrayed. Harmony strays from tradition
enough to be modern, but not troublesome. Usually no
key signatures. Often lyrical. Five pieces use treble
range only, and some passages have only bass range.
Not all children's pieces. Page turns inconvenient.
Spring Water (2) bubbles "gently, lively" with momentary dissonances. Needs facility in interlocking three-
note patterns, which alternate between hands, as well
as in trill-like section, hands together. Silence (4)
has melody of an exquisite line in "moderate, tender"
measures. Threat (5) moves "resolutely quite fast."
Variety of texture includes chords, coupled, and imitative writing. Chords have little preparation time.
Stubborness (9) is spontaneously "perky." Staccato
fourths, fifths, sevenths, polyharmonies and other dissonances hammer out the mood. Rhythm varied by
changing accents and meters shifting from 3/8 to 4/8.
Swift Relay Race (12) has much invention. Excitement
caused by constant motion and intermittent harmonic
clashes. Translations of titles, with directions, are:
Little Flower (1), "moving, tender;" Deep Forest (3),
"quietly, mysteriously;" Joy (6), "not fast;" Grimaces
(7), "lightly, capriciously;" Melancholy (8), "quietly;"
The Little Ballerina (10), "lively;" and Run-Down Clock
(11), "medium fast." (P 11 & p 15.) (MUZ, 1966,
21 pp.) 12 pieces. Ch. 4, some 3 & 5.

4.106 ORTHEL, LÉON. Tre Pezzettini, Op. 42.
Three Small Pieces have splendid taste and assurance.
Approachable, with rare pianistic coloring. Tonal I,
in four sections, alternates between rapid marcato and
delicately tinted slower material. In C, with free use
of all twelve tones. Bright bitonal Poco allegretto II
has rapid finger staccato and some bell-like elements.
III is a Poco lento with deeply felt treble "singing melody," making much from little. Melody of small steps
including augmented seconds over tonic pedal and slightly changing gentle dissonances. (Don, 1958, 5 pp.)
MM, Ped. 5, 6 & 4.

4.107 OSBORNE, WILLSON. Evening Fields.
Lovely. In aeolian and dorian modes. Typical 6/8
rhythms. LH double notes (one usually tonic) include
sevenths. Much dependence on pedal. (Pr, 1954, 2
pp.) Fngr, MM, Ped.

4.108 OSBORNE, WILLSON. Two Quiet Songs.
Of serious integrity. In pure aeolian mode, first on
f and second on e. Both in 2/2. Both have legato
LH acc in two parts, using changing finger on held
tones, or holding one part while other moves. Conservative. (Pr, 1965, 1 p & 1 p.) Fngr, MM.

4.109 OVERTON, HALL. A Mood.
"Slow and free" expressive work with gentle originality. Strongly etched rhythmic and lyrical phrasing.
Texture rich with many thirds and sevenths. Remote-
ly tonal, settling only at end in G, although fourth is
raised. (In 4.1, 1 p.) Fngr, MM. Biog.

4.110 PENHERSKI, ZBIGNIEW. Kolorowe Etiudy (1961).
Studies in Color are moderate and pleasant. Securely
skillful with mild innovations. Traditional forms always return to first material. Rhythms are flexible,
with repeated patterns not agreeing with meter, and
fragments of acc in middle of the beat. Pianistic.
Whimsical 3, an Allegretto moderato, has rhythmically displaced melody and a perpetual motion three-beat
acc pattern. Equal hand emphasis. Rapid thumb-under practice. 4 is an Andante molto cantabile reverie.
Voices change flexibly between one, two and three.
Tonal, only because of repeating bass tone. (PWM,
1965, 8 pp.) 5 pieces. Fngr. 4 & 5.

4.111 PENTLAND, BARBARA. Space Studies.
Appealing studies in "rhythm and compass." Abstract
aims realized clearly. Subtitles and playing directions
very revealing. Twelve-tone, with exception of Quest.
In Space is "study in use of pedal for connecting wide-
spaced melody and for vibration of overtones to enrich
harmony." Melody inverted for last half. Quest, "a
study in contrapuntal phrasing," has two voices.
Phrases are either much shorter in one voice, or en-
tries are staggered. Both invertible counterpoint and
melody inversion for last half. The one five-finger
position for each hand is mirror of the other. (Wat,
1968, 5 pp.) 5 pieces. MM, Ped. *Anal. 4, some
3.

4.112 PERSICHETTI, VINCENT. Little Piano Book, Op. 60.
Contemporary tonal harmony and counterpoint help ex-
pand listening boundaries. Several fast works are
particularly successful for their high spirits. Most
will challenge those steeped in old ways, but two or
three should bother no one. Suitable for the thoughtful
child, as well as for adults. Irresistible Presto
Masque has five-finger or trill-like melody. LH has
staccato ostinato alternation between minor seconds
and major sevenths. Only white keys used. Arietta,
marked Alla recitativo, is unbarred. Improvisatory
melody has little relationship with bass which slowly
descends an octave by major thirds. Outlandish harmonic progressions depict Humoreske, marked Allegretto. Bitonal tendencies. Gay melody has consistent and traditional rhythm. Adagio pesante Prologue
has clear ff polytriads at beginning and ending; in
middle, voice leading determines harmony. Andantino
Canon for two voices uses opening material three
times, in C, B, and C again; in between, melody modulates frequently. Resulting counterpoint sometimes
consonant, sometimes dissonant with polychords. De-
mands of fugal style and voice leading outweigh traditional harmonic niceties in the Fugue. Forearm
strokes used in the non-legato subject of lydian leaning. Includes legato episodes and a stretto. Well-
named Gloria sounds medieval because of chord roots
second apart. (EV, 1954, 15 pp.) 14 pieces.

4.113 PODEŠVA, JAROMÍR. Klavír Říká Říkadla.
Piano Rhymes are accessible works of integrity.
Rhyming poems precede each work in Czech or Slovak

by Josefa Kainara. Tonal (one is modal), with moderate exploration of all twelve tones. Gracefully pianistic, only a few octaves. Allegro assai Barber (p 5)
begins with lyrical bass melody in 2/4, then in 3/8
for closing section. Middle section development stems
from accompanying broken fourths. Soccer (p 8) indicates game's ruggedness in middle section by bass
parallel fifths and rotary acc figure; acc involves three-
tone chord with minor second. Attractive Allegro co-
modo Report Card (p 12), using lydian mode or chromatic tonal harmony, fulfills useful pianistic needs:
rapid near-five-finger passages alternate between hands;
melody played with inner fingers while outer fingers
have repeated tones. Some mirror writing in double
thirds. Translations are Train (p 7), Behind the Rail-
road Station (p 9), Fish (p 10), and Horse and Frogs
(p 11). (PAN, 1964, 10 pp.) 7 pieces. Fngr, Ped.
Ch.

4.114 PROSTAKOFF, JOSEPH. Parade.
Mood of this Allegretto set by many forthright melodic
fourths. Forearm staccato thirds play important part.
Splendidly integrated contemporary approach to tonality,
with incidental polyharmony. (In 4.1, 1 p.) Fngr.

4.115 RADIĆ, DUŠAN. Rondino.
Striking harmonic coloring in Allegro tempo. Mixolydian tune in C, A-flat, G, and E. Alberti bass acc
sometimes has lowered second degree. All in treble
range. (In 4.12, 2 pp.) Fngr, MM. *Biog.

4.116 RAITSCHEV, ALEXANDER. The Angry Rooster and
        The Old Watermill.
Much alternation between two meters needs counting.
Melody and harmony of fourths. Prestissimo, raucous
Angry Rooster has lively and original invention. Par-
allel moving harmonic fifths and seventh chords. The
Old Water Mill (Andante) has free parallel triads.
Two-measure ground bass heard throughout. (In 4.3,
3 pp & 2 pp.) *Biog. 5 & 4.

4.117 RATHAUS, KAROL. Echo.
Open-sounding rubato Allegretto con moto. Flow of
varied ideas. Title depicted literally, and by lower,
softer and related fragments. Coupled writing. Tonal.
(In 4.1, 1 p.) Fngr, MM, some Ped.

4.118 REIN, WALTER. Sonatine in C.
Well-constructed traditional forms. Very German,
medieval influence evident. Conservative. "Lively
and vigorous" first movement has RH rapid passage
work--no thumb-under. Sonata form. In C, mostly
traditional harmonies. Theme and five variations have
some medieval harmonies, as in last two measures of
theme. Fine variety of technical requirements: legato chords, imitation, legato repeated notes, etc.
Theme marked "slow," Var I "moving," II "lightly
moving" and "always sustained," III "very tender and
peaceful," IV "moving" and "most decidedly" and V
"calmer." Rondino marked "joyfully animated." (Ton,
1957, 10 pp.) 3 movements.

4.119 RICHMAN, ALICE. The Meadow Lark.
Lovely music. Pure phrygian mode on e. Added-
note chords arranged with many fourths and fifths in
each hand. Hands skip some to next double notes.
Simplest of rhythms. Good pedal and tone study. Poem is attached. (JF 9571, 1964, 3 pp.) Fngr, MM,
Ped.

4.120 RICHMAN, ALICE. Water Lilies.
Sensitive pastel. Phrygian mode on e. In two-voice
treble, melody is played with weaker fingers. Some
LH extensions and finger reaching over thumb. Good
pedal study. (JF 9161, 1959, 2 pp.)

4.121 RIEGGER, WALLINGFORD. Petite Etude, Op. 62.
Fluency, humor, and fine flair. Atonal technique easily absorbed; also a kind of polytonality with LH on
black and RH on white keys. Develops evenness between hands in rapid, two-note alternations. (Mer,
1957--also in 4.2, 3 pp.) Fngr. *Anal.

4.122 RIISAGER, KNUDÅGE. Den Artige Dreng and Den
      Uartige Pige.
The Well-Mannered Boy is sedate music in aeolian
mode. Usually in two voices. Spontaneous The Ill-
Mannered Girl is "rather impudent" with sforzandos,
staccatos and kaleidoscopic tonal harmonies. Middle
section "smoother." End is "tangy again." Some
coupled writing. (In 6.6, 1 p & 1 p.) Some Fngr,
MM. Biog. 4 & 5.

4.123 RODRIGO, JOAQUIN.   Le Petit Marchand de "chan-
      quêtes."
      An unusually authentic Spanish mood for this level of
      difficulty in The Little Chanquete Seller.   (Footnote by
      composer reports: "The chanquete is a kind of small
      fish caught on the seashore near Malaga, much liked
      when fried.   The second section, marked 'molto rit-
      mico' is a dance typical of region of Malaga in Anda-
      lusia.")   Dissonant snap comes from harmonic major
      and minor seconds, as well as from broken chord out-
      lining major seventh.   RH cantabile melody accom-
      panied by measured trill.   Meter changes from 3/4 to
      6/8; latter includes beat divided by two as well as
      measure divided by three.   (In 5.2, 2 pp.)   Fngr.
      Biog.

4.124 ROGERS, BERNARD.   Bells.
      Intriguing for impressionistic sonorities.   Adventurous
      tonal harmonies in wide keyboard range.   Requires
      fine balance on two and three-tone chords.   Very slow.
      Moves from pp to mf to ppp.   (Pr, 1957, 2 pp.)
      Fngr, MM, Ped.   *Anal.

4.125 RUBBRA, E.   Peasant Dance.
      Vigorous, marked "quickly."   LH acc entirely open
      fifths, often legato with stepwise alternations.   Treble
      melody, using strong fingers, has scale passages (no
      thumb-under) with fifth and fourth fingers well exer-
      cised.   Hand contractions found.   In F/f and a.   Con-
      servative.   (In 4.11 and Five by Ten, Vol. 3, pub. by
      Lengnick, nd, 2 pp.)   Fngr, MM, Ped.

4.126 RUEFF, JEANINE.   Vacances, Vol. 1.
      Holidays is an excellent introduction to music of its
      kind.   Neo-romantic and conservative.   Works serve
      as pleasant introduction to chromatic excursions and
      modulations at an uncommonly easy level.   Collection
      balanced between very calm and allegretto, moderate-
      ly extrovert numbers.   Two titles might restrict vol-
      ume to children alone.   Two modal numbers.   Octave
      reach used.   Swing (3) is one-line, moderate tempo
      music.   Hands alternate between broken triads often
      half tone apart.   Pim, the Fine Pony (5) is jolly.   Be-
      gins in g, succeeded by g-sharp.   Last chord includes
      added major sixth and seventh.   The Flowers Dance
      (6) has treble lyric melody with important appoggia-
      turas.   Many seventh and ninth chords, as well as

chromatic harmonies.   LH has finger-over-thumb in
broken chords.   Typical rhythms of 6/8 meter in the
Andantino On the Fine River (8).   Harmonies often
parallel.   RH melody mildly extended.   Title translations are We Will Go to the Woods (1), An Old Nanny
Sings (2), Catichou the Cat Is Sad (4), Rest Under the
Big Trees (7), Let's Visit the Old Castle (9), and Jazz
(10).   (Led, 1968, 12 pp.)   10 pieces.   MM.   4 & 5.

4.127 SAEVERUD, HARALD.   Sonatina, Op. 30, No. 3.
Aim of highest intent, impeccable craftsmanship.
Sensitive, with refined subjectivity.   Tonal, with free
use of all twelve tones.   In two-part texture.   Allegretto grazioso securely directs ebb and flow of tension
and release through ritards, accelerandos, and changes
of temp.   Andante's RH melody heard twice with different harmonizations: second time adds bass range with
surprising intoning of tonic tone.   Much subtle detail.
(In 6.5, 3 pp.)   2 movements.   MM.   4 & 5.

4.128 SALTER, LIONEL.   Spooks.
"Misterioso" novelty number with many technical benefits.   Tonal, with chromaticism and diminished seventh
chords.   Among techniques used are (a) grace notes
and chords with different hands as well as other quick
hand exchanges, (b) hand staccato chromatic scales, and
(c) diminished seventh arpeggios, particularly in LH.
Varied range.   Texture diversified by coupled writing.
(Ric-L, 1963, 2 pp.)   1 min, 20 sec.   Some Fngr,
MM, Ped.   Ch.

4.129 SANTA CRUZ, DOMINGO.   Childhood Images, Series
        One, Opus 13a.
Undemonstrative works of quiet character, possibly
memories of childhood by grown-up, surely not for
most children.   Polyharmonies often implied.   Titles
also in Spanish.   Haunting While the Grown-Up People
Talk is marked Tranquillo e monotono.   Melody, sometimes in first five tones of phrygian mode, has chromatic harmonization.   Some stepwise sixths or sevenths.
Texture has two, three or four melodic voices.   What
the Dwarf Said to Me is told "with joy" and brightness.
Polyharmony used.   In two voices, with LH usually
rapid "equal" five-finger ostinato and RH a rapid melody with irregular accents.   (Peer, 1960, 5 pp.)   4
pieces.   MM.   4, some 5 & 6.

4.130 SATIE, ERIK. Carnet d'Esquisses et de Croquis.
Notebook of Sketches and Outlines, along with other
Satie works reviewed (see 4.131, 4.132, 5.123, 5.124,
5.125, 5.126 and 5.127) were first published forty-
three years after his death in 1925. It is hardly like-
ly that these are comparable to that master's piano
works long since published. Their musical characteristics are more conservative than others in this Guide,
but since publication was delayed until 1968, they are
included.

Rich variety in the twenty pieces in Notebook. Robert
Caby, reviser of the works, writes in preface in
French that they are like certain published sketches of
painters. He has "eliminated the rough drafts of the
well known pieces, as well as the scholastic exercises
except for a few interesting and personal studies."
Works range from an incomplete fragment of twelve
measures to a pleasant two-page contrapuntal Exercise
and a two-page obvious Little Prelude from the Death
of Mr. Fly from Sketches and Outlines from Montmartre (p 13). Simple three-voice treble Exercise (p
5) is in strong contrast to Little Prelude with its rapid back-and-forth LH octave acc. Harmonies is a bar-
less, keyless, fifteen-chord progression in quarter
notes. Voice leading determines the chords. (In all
numbers, care for contrapuntal motion is apparent.)
Chant (p 7) is a dense Largo using as many as eight
voices. Second of the Montmartre Sketches (p 15) is
downright tuneful. Simplest of harmonies. Acc
rhythms usually an eighth, two sixteenths and two
eighths. Elegant Little Dance (p 16) is marked "gaily."
Two measure by two measure construction. Basically
in two treble voices, with some filling out into chords.
Translations are Essay (p 2), The Sullen Prisoner and
Sketches "The Grand Ape" (p 4), Reverie About "Jack"
from the "Airs Urging You to Flee" (p 6), Scraps (p
7), and Essays--Secret Words (p 16). (Sal, 1968, 15
pp.) 20 pieces, 12 min. 4 & 5, some 2, 3 & 6.

4.131 SATIE, ERIK. Douze Petits Chorals.
(See 4.130.) Concerning Twelve Little Chants, R.
Caby, who has revised the music, writes in preface in
French: "... a dense and heavy music in which the
harmonic and contrapuntal qualities, excluding any intention of further development, reaches a high degree
of intensity conforming to the esthetic nature of his

very condensed musical thought." Factually, nine
chants are tonal; three modal; five are quite chromatic;
eight are strictly for four voices (some octave doubling)
and four freely add voices for fullness; two have wide-
spread voices requiring broken playing; and three are
without bar lines. (Sal, 1968, 6 pp.) 4, some 3.

4.132 SATIE, ERIK. Rêverie du Pauvre (1900).
(See 4.130.) Reverie of the Pauper (for a time Satie
referred to himself as Monsieur le Pauvre) is solemn
chordal study to be played "with a humble and gentle
simplicity." Slow motion by half notes. From two to
five-tone chords in RH; often no LH. In D-flat, with
intermediate cadences in e-flat. Some modal cadences.
Revision by R. Caby. (Sal, 1968, 2 pp.) 4 min, 5
sec. MM.

4.133 SAYGUN, A. ADNAN. Inci's Book.
Has Eastern flavor, musical simplicity and purity.
Masterly organization. Pure modal influences. Three
works have no black keys, others have very few.
Three in treble range only. LH has broken chords
spread out to ninths, infrequently to tenths and elevenths
no two tones held. Giocoso and rapid Playful Kitten
flows along naturally. Splendid unity between broken
chord melody and near-ostinato acc. Equal hand emphasis. Some extensions. In pure C. Tale, with
mildly ornate or chantlike melody, has "misterioso"
mood. RH concentrated melody uses isolated sixteenths
before and on the beat, as well as sextolet of sixteenths. LH cluster chords up to four tones. In aeolian on a and e. Giant Puppet, extrovert and convincing, has one texture of coupled writing and another
with drone bass. In dorian on d and g. (SMP, 1952,
9 pp.) 7 pieces. MM. Ch. 4, some 3.

4.134 SCHICKELE, PETER. Three Folk Settings.
Most appropriate settings of two fast and one slow
modal folk tunes. Melodies always in treble; composer
sometimes tastefully adds to tunes. Swashbuckling
Henry Martin the most adventurous because one section
has low chromatic triads in cross rhythm. Poignant
Turtle Dove gives practice for pedal, lyrical tone and
two voices in LH, with longer tones for one voice.
Mixolydian Old Joe Clark has play between major and
minor third degrees. Hand staccato. Alberti bass.
(EV, 1963, 6 pp.)

4.135 SCHLOSS, JULIUS.   Twenty-Three Pieces.
"For children in twelve-tone style." Very musical,
with genuine merit. Many expression marks. Infrequent chords usually have only two tones. Consistent
in difficulty. Twelve-tone system easy to analyze.
Same set used in Pieces 1, 2, 7, 11, 13, 14, 16, 18,
19, 20 and 21.   Repetitions help inexperienced listener
of twelve-tone music.   Titles often apt for the music,
such as Follow the Leader, Raindrops, Undecided,
Crowded, Chimes, Odd, Feeling Blue, Determination
and Ping Pong.   Traditional methods of composition
are found: imitation in Scherzo and Spook; recogniz-
able motives in March and Remembering, as well as
motto motive in Out of the Depths; common chords in
A Picture, as well as cluster chords in The Turtle
and the Hare; fourths in Study in Fourths; invertible
counterpoint in Going Places, The Soloist and Valse
Triste; logical development in Let's Go and Walking.
Homage to Chopin is remarkably like his e minor
Prelude.   Among technical features: extensions in
Follow the Leader and Going Places; tone study in
Homage to Chopin, The Soloist and Valse Triste;
three-note chords in Homage to Chopin and March;
rapid hand alternation in Odd and Ping Pong; and
double notes in Fourths and Determination.   (Peer,
1958 & 1965, 20 pp.)   Ch.   4, some 3 & 5.

4.136 SCHLOSS, JULIUS.   Twenty-Three Studies.
"For children in twelve-tone style." (See 4.135 for
general comments.) Appears to be no difference in
works whether titled Studies or Pieces, as in 4.135.
Same tone set mentioned in Pieces used in Studies 1,
2, 4, 6, 8, 13, 18, 20 and 21.   Apt titles in Horns,
I Told You So, Bad Dream, Why? and Too Close.
Traditional composition methods found: invertible
counterpoint in Strife and De Profundis; logical development in Coming Along, Problems and Polka; varied
repetition in Dreaming, Hesitation, A Song and Lady of
Mystery; ostinato in People; and formal repetition in
Teasing Brother J.   Waltz and Hornpipe quite traditional.   Among technical features: rapid two-note slurs in
Rush Hour, Keep Going and Continuation; forearm staccato in Polka and Teasing Brother J.; hand staccato in
Horns and People; and flexible wrist in Coming Along
and Melody.   (Peer, 1962 & 1965, 24 pp.)   Ch. 4,
some 3 & 5.

4.137 SCHMIDT, Y. RUDNER. <u>Caipirinha Triste</u> (1967).
<u>Sad Little Hillbilly</u>, marked "sorrowful," is very con-
servative. In a, with harmony usually three principal
triads. Few extensions in LH melody, which "stands
out, but softly." RH takes some small leaps with skillful secondary ideas. (IVi, 1968, 2 pp.) Fngr, Ped.

4.138 SCHRAMM, HAROLD. <u>Bharata Sangita</u>.
Melody-oriented <u>Indian Music</u> "is a set of original piano
compositions, conceived as a synthesis of Eastern and
Western musical elements...." Useful pieces employ
pentatonic, double harmonic and dorian modes, among
others not identified. Added to characteristic augmented seconds is chromaticism, with ascending lines often
raised and vice versa. Numerous meter changes, measures with one beat, and phrases ending on subdivisions
of beat. Simple accs, with some preference for chord
with broken fifth and ninth. Included is a <u>Suite</u> with
seven attacca numbers. <u>Prelude</u> has overlapping two-
note slurs progressing by step. Texture changes to
passages without pedal. <u>Etude</u> begins and ends with section in pentatonic mode; melody has interesting separated and combined fragments. LH has characteristic
rhythm in middle section. RH has rapid passages
throughout. Delightfully extrovert <u>Rondo</u> has recurring
pattern of 4/4, 3/4 and 5/4; interesting for offbeat acc,
tied and syncopated tones in melody. Some inversion of
melody in last half. Many melodic augmented seconds.
(MCA, 1965, 18 pp.) 6 pieces. MM, Ped. Anal. 4
& 5.

4.139 SCHRAMM, HAROLD. <u>Kiravani-Ramapriya</u>.
Genuine exotic appeal for Westerners in <u>Lotus</u> Dance.
Title refers to two South Indian ragas, as explained by
composer. Melody includes all twelve tones in the octave. Varied treble melody defines six sections, one
repeating and another developing a previous section.
Drone acc uses "tonic" played by fifth finger and shorter
"dominant" played by thumb. Some rhythms of three
against two. (AME, 1965, 3 pp.) Anal.

4.140 SCHULMAN, ALAN. <u>One Man Show</u>.
Attractive works of invention and variety. Rhythmically
and harmonically alive. All are tonal or modal. Humorous <u>Dialogue</u> really talks! RH has G hand staccato
broken triads only; single-tone LH has much pentatonic
mode on black keys. Both voices start and stop in en-

gaging fitfulness. Slow-paced <u>Winter Day</u> creates mood
with repetitive melody and ostinatolike acc, its repeated low tone good practice for not looking at keyboard.
<u>Mischief</u> aptly depicted by brief frolics of volatile har-
mony and unpredictable 2/2 rhythms. Three-note motive may end accented or unaccented. Diminished fifth
wins out over perfect fifth. <u>The Mexican Mountain</u>
<u>Climb</u> has one intricate rhythm in which LH is grouped
by three plus three plus two, while RH has broken triads ascending or descending by unchanging threes. Another rhythm has simpler syncopation. (P 14.) (Fox,
1962, 16 pp.) 9 pieces. MM.

4.141 SCHUMAN, WILLIAM. <u>Three Piano Moods: II Pen-</u>
      <u>sive</u> (1958).
      Decidedly individual. Needs emotional maturity.
      Chromatic, obscurely tonal harmony explained in analy-
      sis. Excellent for finger legato in four-part texture.
      (Mer, 1958, 2 pp.) Fngr, MM. *Anal.

4.142 SHLONSKY, VERDINA. <u>Youth Suite</u>.
      Naturally musical and most sincere. Often modal. In
      two-voice texture, melody and countermelody. Moder-
      ate ranges. Suitable for all ages. <u>A Story</u> is a quiet-
      ly singing molto moderato, mostly in aeolian mode.
      LH countermelody almost as active as melody. <u>Dance</u>
      is sturdy ben ritmato with regular and irregular ac-
      cents, and varied articulations, including forearm stac-
      cato. In aeolian and mixolydian modes on c. Dark
      key of f serves well for grave mood in <u>Complaint</u>.
      Acc thirds striking for chromatic dissonances, accents
      and rhythmic shape; played both legato and staccato.
      (ICL, 1965, 9 pp.) 7 pieces. 4 & 5.

4.143 SLUKA, LUBOŠ. <u>Hry a Sny</u>.
      <u>Games and Dances</u> are pleasant. Divided equally be-
      tween pastel lyrics and nimble novelties, latter partic-
      ularly useful for rapid LH. Traditional except for
      moderate chromaticisms. Titles in Czech and German.
      <u>In the Shade</u> (1) has treble melody of three-measure
      phrases. LH acc has chromatic thirds, with lovely
      cross relations. Ends with tonic minor seventh chord.
      (<u>In the Swing</u> (2) is in 4.144, described there as <u>A</u>
      <u>Merry Piece</u>.) Presto possibile <u>Echo</u> (4) is facile
      etude for LH fingers circling around thumb; simultan-
      eous RH five-finger melody. For rhythmic contrast,
      RH has accented groupings of three against LH continu-

ing fours. At Twilight (5) sweetly sentimental. In A.
LH first inversion broken chord acc colored by some
chromaticism. Title translations are Good Night (3),
The Cuckoo (6), The Dragon-Fly (7), and Bells (8).
(Sup, 1966, 9 pp.) 8 pieces. Fngr, MM, Ped. 4 &
5, some 3.

4.144 SLUKA, LUBOŠ. Two Merry Pieces for Piano.
First Piece (scherzando) is high-spirited trifle of chro-
matic harmonic charm. (Also in 4.143, titled there
In the Swing.) Rapid hand alternation with RH offbeat
acc. Metronome marking seems about twice too slow.
Second Piece, like jolly folk dance, has captivating
chromaticisms. Expressive nonharmonic tones. Live-
ly articulations. ABA in form with varied settings for
A material. Conservative. (In 4.7, 1 p & 4 pp.)
Fngr, MM, Ped. 4 & 5.

4.145 SMITH, HALE. Faces of Jazz.
Jazz qualities sure and subtle, with striking harmonic
richness. Solid substance with economical means.
My Scarf is Yellow is played loosely but "crisply."
First there is three-beat LH pattern against changing
RH pattern; second section has syncopated accents and
rests, as well as harmonies built up to eleventh chords.
In Pooty's Blues LH has two-bar ground bass, RH
mostly harmonic thirds with grace notes. Expressive
Day's End, marked "slow--quietly singing," has slowly
changing cluster chords in bass. Many phrases end
on dissonances. Title Off-Beat Shorty indicates its
rhythmic character. Syncopated and repeated harmonic
pattern moves by steps in contrary motion to dominant
or tonic harmonies. Scrambled Eggs and Ernie moves
in an "easy swing--not too fast." Dotted rhythms, triplets and walking bass. Ends with submediant triad over
tonic; includes added minor seventh. Texture in That's
Mike starts with coupled writing, adds parallel RH
chords, and climaxes with full chords in each hand.
Irresistible rhythm in "moderate swing." Rests important. In c. (Mrk, 1968, 16 pp.) 12 pieces.
Some Fngr, MM, some Ped. 4, some 5.

4.146 SMITH-MASTERS, ANTHONY. Quiet Dance.
"Leisurely" and pleasant. Uses lydian mode, but ostinato pattern ends on lowered seventh. 5/4 meter.
More active two-part texture in middle section. Cultivates RH weak-finger singing tone with double notes.

Conservative. (Ric-L, 1959, 2 pp.) Fngr, MM.

4.147 STARER, ROBERT. Above, Below and Between.
In this witty "fast and light" number main material
shows lyrical jazz influences. Polytonal staccato interludes. Title refers to positions of hands in relation to each other. Thin textures. (In 4.1, 3 pp.)
Some Fngr.

4.148 STARER, ROBERT. Seven Vignettes.
Variety between works of immediate appeal and some
more severe. Usually tonal, with wide-ranging harmonies. No more than three tones used at same time.
Song Without Words is a beauty! Repeated acc of
double notes of all dimensions except octaves used for
pastel coloring. End has striking parallel sevenths.
The Interrupted Waltz lyrically attractive. Has slurs
across the beat, syncopations, and phrase endings on
weak beats. LH double notes always move chromatically, either in oblique or contrary motion. In Toccata, rapid eighths alternate between hands until they
skip to widely spaced, three-tone dissonant jabs. In
C, with free use of all twelve tones. (P 5.) (Leeds-
NY, 1950, 10 pp.) 4, some 5.

4.149 STARER, ROBERT. Sketches in Color.
Accessible. In fine preface composer agrees that nam-
ing of pieces by color is "arbitrary at best," and con-
cludes that "they may also be performed without their
titles." Various aspects of contemporary music named
in preface pass in review. Marked "slow, with intensity," the expressive Purple alternates between low
polychords (LH only fourths or fifths) and widely-
spaced coupled writing. "Fast and light" Bright Orange
spontaneously employs parallel triads moving by step
and jazz syncopations, first beats anticipated. Color
stressed with garish climax on c-sharp. High-spirited
Crimson moves "fast and hard" in 7/8, with beats
grouped by four and three. Fine opportunity for RH
hand staccato on repeated tones or chords. Vivid dynamics. (Leeds-NY, 1964, 9 pp.) 7 pieces. Some
Fngr, MM. 4 & 5.

4.150 STARER, ROBERT. The Telegraph.
Spontaneous. Played "as fast as you can." Moves
from E-flat to g-sharp to C. Splendid for independent
hands on two lines and for fast repeated tones in either

hand. (Pr, 1956, 2 pp.) Fngr. *Anal.

4.151 STEIN, LEON. Melody.
An accessible Moderato. Sometimes modal, sometimes
polytonal, such as B and A-flat together. Equal hand
emphasis. Useful for singing touch and for hand staccato on broken chord acc. (Mer, 1957, 2 pp.) Fngr.
*Anal.

4.152 SZELÉNYI, ISTVÁN. Melody and Canon, Squabble,
       and Faraway Regions.
Plaintive Andante melody in first number is heard three
times, last time in canon. Has stepwise motion and
much internal organization. Equal hand use, simplest
thumb-under technique. In phrygian mode on a.
Squabble attractively disguises trill exercise for all
fingers. Mirror motion, hands alone and together.
Dynamic variety. Dorian mode on d. Faraway Re-
gions is atmospheric work in whole tone scale, played
"harmoniously lento." While pedal holds a five-note
rolled chord, melody is "far away, without any expression." Successive beats divided by five, six and eight.
(In 4.8--also last 2 in 1.5, each 1 p.) Fngr. 2 & 4
& 4.

4.153 SZERVÁNSZKY, ENDRE. Etude.
An ingenious study. Stronger and weaker fingers alternate between important held tones and shorter trill-like
acc. Hands are equal. In phrygian mode on g, but
with raised third at cadences. (In 4.8, 2 pp.) Fngr.

4.154 TARDOS, BÉLA. Rainbow.
Especially notable for three polytonal novelty numbers.
Articulations varied in Molto vivace The Funny Trum-
peter. Tune often centered on dominant of B while LH
acc repeats strong fifths and sixths mostly on A. Other harmonic wanderings as well make piece humorous.
Cater-Wauling is hilarious. LH staccato pentatonic
melody centered on C-sharp, while underneath, RH
maintains constant white-key chatter with rapid five-
finger and scale passages. Hurrah is like a Presto
con bravura toccata. LH on black and RH on white
keys sound like parallel motion first inversion triads
with double inflections. Hands often alternate. Titles
also in Hungarian and German. (Pp 2, 3 & 6, No. 5.)
(EMB, 1959, 10 pp.) 7 pieces. Fngr, MM. 4, 6 &
7.

4.155 TCHEREPNIN, ALEXANDER.   Mic and Mac (1954).
Spontaneous.   Played "with animation."   Bite of one
character's sforzando minor seconds and sweetness of
other's tenths provide contrast.   Often coupled writing
by octaves or tenths.   Broken chord melody challenging.   Conservative.   (In 4.6, 2 pp.)   Fngr.

4.156 TCHEREPNIN, ALEXANDER.   Valse, Merry-Go-
        Round and Old Tale.
Valse pleasant lyrical piece in A in treble range.
Traditional texture, LH holds tone (counter melody)
through each measure, repeating tonic tone on beats
two and three.   Conservative.   Merry-Go-Round enchanting music-box piece.   Melody in duple meter
while acc is in triple.   In F, only one accidental.
Hands treated equally.   Broken chord perpetual motion acc uses hand staccato.   Conservative.   Old Tale
sounds Russian, with advantages of both lyricism and
faster staccato playing.   Begins in dorian mode with
melody in coupled setting two octaves apart.   In twice-
faster section one hand has repeated hand staccato
pedal tone, while other has double notes in groups of
eight eighth notes--three plus three plus two.   (In 3.5,
1 p, 2 pp, 1 p.)   Fngr, some Ped.

4.157 TOCH, ERNST.   Reflections, Op. 86.
Witty play with sounds.   Neo-classic.   Always pianistic, usually fast and light hearted.   Texture balanced
between polyphony and homophony.   Tonal harmonies
mostly conservative.   I, usually in two equal parts,
develops hand independence and some facility with
groups of short tones.   II is sprightly-mannered Allegretto.   After indecision about key, manages to end on
C-sharp; hints of polyharmony and augmented intervals
add piquancy.   IV, often using four-part chords, has
modal progressions.   (MIL-NY, 1962, 5 pp.)   5
pieces.   MM.   4 & 5.

4.158 URBANNER, ERICH.   11 Bagatellen.
Bagatelles are miniatures in twelve-tone technique.
Expressive aims of medium difficulty, but emotional
flexibility needed.   Rests important.   Dynamic contrasts are cultivated.   Medium wide range.   Usually
no more than double notes.   Preface in English and
German.   II wittily repeats two and three-note set segments, with p and f contrasts.   Often only one line.
Gentleness of IV, Andante con espressivo, attained

by use of melodic and harmonic sixth and thirds. VII,
marked marcatissimo, is one-line music, mostly in
quarter note jabs. Two tempos are possible, one
twice faster. Allegro IX rhythmically fanciful, unified
by constant presence of two acc tones. Rhythmic variety in Moderato X. (UE 13165, 1961, 8 pp.) MM.
4 & 5.

4.159 WAGENAAR, BERNARD. The Flickering Candle.
Sensitive work has stately melody, supported by three-
tone cluster chords. In key of c-sharp with gentle
color changes. Hands have equal opportunities. Sex-
tolets included. Useful for soft dynamic control. (Pr,
1958--also in 4.2, 2 pp.) *Anal.

4.160 WAGENAAR, BERNARD. Saltarello.
Of a rollicking gaiety. Much rapid five-finger passage
work (sometimes divided between hands) will need care
for smoothness. In two-part texture. LH in D-flat,
RH in C. (Pr, 1957, 2 pp.) Fngr. *Anal.

4.161 WARD-STEINMAN, DAVID. Improvisations on Children's Songs (1964, 1966).
A good idea! Harmonizations challenge hearing habits,
disputing "right" way to set a tune. Each tune has
two, three, and four settings. Many contemporary
techniques applied: Twinkle, Twinkle Little Star uses
parallel harmonies over pedal tone, as well as poly-
haromonies; Happy Birthday to You also has polyharmonies, as well as added-note chords; Frère Jacques
uses changing meters and amusing pointillism. At
times tunes are obscured. (LR, 1967, 5 pp.) 3
pieces, 3 min, 45 sec. Fngr, MM, Ped. Ch. 4 & 5.

4.162 WARD-STEINMAN, DAVID. Three Miniatures (1964).
These change from conservative to more contemporary.
Composer offers optional readings for less difficulty.
Rustic Dance mostly traditional. Sudden dynamic and
key changes depict title. Lovely Song, in 5/4, gives
legato practice in three-part playing. "Very fast" City
Dance wonderfully spontaneous. Rhythm irregular with
unexpected accents and rests. Two-part texture (one
a repeated tone), also chordal texture where dissonant
triads are noticeable. (LR, 1965, 4 pp.) Fngr. 4 &
5.

4.163 WAXMAN, DONALD. Second Recital Pageant.
Strikes judicious balance between immediate appeal and
skillful craftsmanship. Tonal. Moderate range explorations. Subtitled "A Natural History for Piano."
Perhaps titles not for teenagers, but music is. Conservatively contemporary. Grasshopper on the Go
progresses with admirable unity and variety. RH has
many two, three, and four-note chords. LH acc
sometimes uses hand staccatos, other times slight extensions. ABA in form, with contrast of B-flat and
A tonalities but same melodic material in B. Tranquillo, adagietto Lone Firefly is lovely. Fine for
rotary motion on broken chords, sometimes as full as
eleventh chords. Polychordal suggestions. Requires
soft equal dynamics. The Trained Seal must have
training of performer because of interesting differences
from the norm. 4/4 meter shifts to 8/8 with LH
melody groupings of three plus three plus two. Key
wavers between F and f, often has raised dominant,
and modulates frequently. (Galx, 1963, 13 pp.) 6
pieces. Fngr, MM, Ped. 4, some 5.

4.164 WEBERN, ANTON von. Kinderstück (1924).
Charming Children's Piece, marked "pleasing." Dis-
covered very recently. Strictest twelve-tone writing.
Nearly every tone in different register from preceding
tone; hence, typical of Webern. Detailed dynamic directions never louder than mp. (CF, 1966, 1/4 p.)
*Anal.

4.165 WILLIAMSON, MALCOLM. Travel Diaries, Vol. 1,
Sydney.
Attractive short pieces which fit programmatic titles
with pleasing aptness and taste. Modernisms are
slight. Each piece technically consistent. Probably
most appealing to early teenagers, then children. In
each of the five volumes (see 4.166, 4.167, 5.156 and
6.168) last piece is first piece in reverse. Explana-
tions of titles, when needed. "Craggy eminence" of
North Head depicted by dissonances of bitonality, reiterated fifths with and without added second, and repeated tones. At Central Railway generates excitement by increasing and diminishing dynamics and slow
bass trills. Hand staccato requires endurance. Har-
bour Ferry, a traditional waltz, begins with LH melody. In central section acc assigned to thumbs of
each hand. Lane Cove is in pentatonic mode on black

keys. Practice for soft, evenly balanced LH on four-
note ostinatolike acc. Swinging Allegro King's Cross
has only parallel added-sixth chords. Jazz rhythm of
anticipated second beat. Wonder and majesty of The
Southern Cross expressed by staccato melodic fourths,
progressing as far as six ascending fourths, continual
meter changes, and bass ostinato of two chords.
(Chap-L 45907, 1962, 11 pp.) 13 pieces. Fngr, MM,
Ped. *Anal. 4, some 3.

4.166 WILLIAMSON, MALCOLM. Travel Diaries, Vol. 2,
    Naples.
(See 4.165.) Descriptions confined to solo works although six duets for student and teacher included,
where student's parts are easier than in four solos of
collection. The graceful Bay of Naples (Arrival) has
scalelike melody in LH. RH uses rotary motion on
broken triads, which sometimes complete polyharmonies. Hands alternate rapidly on every tone in the
ff Presto Railway Station. Needs strong hand staccato.
Allegro Shopping in the Via Roma useful for hand independence. RH melody has scales, LH ostinatolike
series of broken parallel triads. In pure F. (Chap-
L 45906, 1962, 14 pp.) 10 pieces. Fngr, Ped.
*Anal.

4.167 WILLIAMSON, MALCOLM. Travel Diaries, Vol. 3,
    London.
(See 4.165.) Music particularly evokes program titles.
Helicopter Station is graceful Allegretto. Coupled writing in thirds makes bitonality. Rhythmic flexibility
and expansion by motivic extension are features. Con
grazia Lunch in St. James's Park is traditional in A
section, has mild harmonic exploration in section B--
all most charming. Naive wonderment beautifully expressed in The Planetarium. Pedal blends legato
thirds, as well as augmented fourths. "... two positions of the whole-tone scale ... are set in conflict."
Along the Mall uses double notes, legato in RH and
staccato in LH ostinato. Traditional English, except
for momentary out-of-key chromaticism. The Royal
Festival Hall offers opportunities for slight lateral extensions in clever staccato tunings of violins, flute,
timpani, etc. (Chap-L 45908, 1962, 12 pp.) 10
pieces. Fngr, MM, Ped. *Anal. 4 & 5.

4.168 ZUPKO, RAMON. Burlesque (1960).
Has fine contrast between sections. First section
melody lively with varied, intricate articulations; in
middle section beautiful lyrical melody has simple
rhythm.   Acc of double notes throughout has steady
staccato strokes often unrelated to melody.   At end,
added-note chords emphasize importance of fourths
and fifths. (LR, 1962, 3 pp.) Fngr, MM.

LEVEL 5

5.1 DESCAVES, LUCETTE, ed. Les Contemporains,
Deuxième Recueil.
Second Collection of The Contemporaries has pianistically deft works useful for exploring accidentals within tonality. Five are reviewed (see 5.48, 5.116,
5.131, 6.10, and 6.35)--others usually too conservative. Preface, in French, by Daniel Lesur "for par-
ents" and "for students." Music by Aubin, Auric,
Bondeville, Delannoy, Dutilleux, Gallois-Montbrun,
Hoerée, Revel, Rivier, Schmit, and Yvain. Titles
usually in French, English, German, and Spanish.
(Bil, 1950, 37 pp.) 11 pieces, 11 composers. Fngr,
some MM, Ped. 5 & 6.

5.2 DESCAVES, LUCETTE, ed. Les Contemporains,
Troisième Recueil.
Third Collection of The Contemporaries is much like
first two collections. Eight works reviewed (see 3.48,
3.77, 3.91, 4.123, 5.49, 5.55, 5.90, and 5.96)--re-
maining too conservative. Contains music by Cortese,
Gagnebin, Genzmer, Harsanyi, Kabalevsky, Katchatur-
ian, Lippe, Marescotti, Martin, Martinu, Poot, Rodrigo, Stubbs, Tansman, and Shostakovich, none of
whom are French. Titles only in French. Two-page
pieces, with one exception. Notes by Daniel Lesur in
French, mostly biographical. (Bil, 1952, 33 pp.) 16
pieces, 16 composers. Some Fngr & MM. Biog. 5,
some 3 & 4.

5.3 International Library of Piano Music, Album 9.
Outstanding choice of composers and works. Covers
Impressionist and Twentieth Century periods. Available only by purchasing entire set of nine albums.
All works first published within the time scope of this
study are reviewed. (See 5.136 and 7.89.) Contains
works by Ravel, Rebikoff, Reger, Riegger, Schönberg,

Scriabin, Sessions, Shostakovitch, Smith, Sorokine,
Stravinsky, Sydeman, Toch, Turina, Villa Lobos, and
Webern. (University Society, 1967, 181 pp.) 40
pieces, 16 composers. Some Fngr, MM & Ped. 5 &
7.

5.4   Sonatinas, Collection I.
Useful volume of Japanese works. Even if works are
eclectic in style, they are skillful and pleasant. Two
works reviewed. (See 5.95 and 5.159.) Contains music by Hara, Ikenouchi, Miyoshi, Okumura, Otaka,
Takagui, Tsukatani, and Yamada. Foreword, comments about music, and some playing directions in
Japanese. (Ongaku, 1967, 104 pp.) 7 Sonatinas & 1
Suite, 8 composers. Some Fngr, MM & Ped.

5.5   Svenska Albumblad 1962.
Swedish Albumleaves, commissioned by publisher,
were written in 1962. Ten works reviewed. (See
5.28, 5.72, 5.83, 5.158, 6.79, 6.80, 6.93, 6.129,
and 7.31.) As pointed out in foreword, pieces are
quiet and of an inward expressiveness, with one exception. Most are mildly contemporary with somewhat
lavish piano sound. Contains music by Carlstedt, De
Frumerie, Eklund, Hallnäs, Johanson, Karkoff, v. Koch,
Larsson, Liljefors, Linde, Rosenberg, and Wirén.
Foreword in Swedish, titles in Swedish and Italian.
(P 8 & 12.) (Geh, 1962, 20 pp.) 12 pieces, 12 composers. Some MM & Ped. 5 & 6, some 7.

5.6   ANDRIESSEN, JURRIAAN. Drie Bagatellen.
Three Bagatelles have romantic expressiveness. Ideas
are short, so their urgency soon ends. Each work admirably unified. Two slow pieces use rubato. Tonality diffused by rich chromaticism. I has a main ex-
pansive idea with harmonization of a third, sixths, and
a second. Imitation used. II is spontaneous, in lyrical lines accompanied by single sforzando strokes, longer polychords, and staccato broken triads. III, wonderfully musical, ends after much chromatic wandering
with sweetest F-sharp chord. (B&VP 816, 1964, 5
pp.)

5.7   APOSTEL, HANS ERICH. Vier kleine Klavierstücke,
       Op. 31a and Fantasie, Op. 31b.
Four Small Piano Pieces and Fantasy are quite accessible for twelve-tone writing. A few familiar chords,

tonal references, and traditional formal procedures. Promenade is two-voice canon by inversion with complex articulations. Middle section relaxed with finch, cuckoo, and quail quotations, alternating with harmonic seconds. March has repetitions of material. More chordal material for the Trio. Fantasy is a very expressive work; appeals with broad sweeping lines (frequently coupled writing) and warm chromatic harmonies. Prodigious variety of strong rhythmic gestures in Largo and somewhat faster tempo. (Dob, 1962, 4 pp & 4 pp.) 6 min, 30 sec & 4 min. 5, 6 & 7.

5. 8   AVSHALOMOV, JACOB. Slow Dance.
"In the manner of an old-world Sarabande." Splendid for RH melody emphasis on weaker fingers in chordal texture and for polyphonic accompanying voices. Has ground bass, although not restricted to bass. In g aeolian and G mixolydian modes. Large reach. (Mer, 1957, 2 pp.) Fngr, MM. *Anal.

5. 9   BACEWICZ, GRAŻYNA. Suita Dziecięca.
Children's Suite is pianistically resourceful. Pleasant works are tastefully expressive (rather French), not difficult to understand. Clearly tonal, with apt and unexpected chromaticism. Traditional rhythms and forms --dances, like Gavotte, etc. Texture always RH melody and LH acc. Allegro ma non troppo Preludium is elegant and gentle. LH has rapid acc figure with much thumb involvement. Lullaby (p 7), marked Moderato tranquillo, uses in both hands outer fingers for melody and bass and inner fingers for faster moving acc. In the Vivo Burleska, LH uses staccato parallel broken chord patterns involving extensions and double notes. Bright-sounding chromatic shifts. Attractive Allegretto Scherzino in keys using several flats or sharps. Forearm strokes on simultaneous double note short slurs in each hand; melody in RH outer fingers. (PWM, 1966, 13 pp.) 8 pieces. Fngr, Ped. 5 & 6, some 7.

5. 10 BACON, ERNST. Byways.
" ... based on folk tunes from many countries." Musical joy of the ages, with musicological worth too. For performers of any age, especially those whose listening habits limit them to customary sounds. Wonderful settings, in the spirit of the tunes, often unconventional. (However, a third of settings are too conservative for this study.) Irrelevant pianistic accumulation

resisted.   The composer has a musical ear and trusts
it.   Repetition of tune usually harmonized differently
or tune may be altogether abandoned.   Music often
modal.   Some helpful playing directions.   Sources included for unfamiliar tunes.   Ten melodies from USA,
three from Scotland, three from Scandinavia, three
from Germany, two from Ireland, etc.   Titles in language of tune's country and usually in English.

Pilgrim Hymn has appropriately "crude" harmonization: frequent parallel fifths (no third) and wider spacing than usual.   Dorian mode on d.   Immer Langsam
Voran has realistic tread; also soldier's roughness
through bass range only and outlandish harmonizations.
Tune's key undeniably C, but piece ends in a.   Tune
of Cavaleer Dandsen is minor, but acc often major.
In two voices only, with distinct rhythm for each
voice.   Sorcery in Den Lillas Testamente is depicted
by tune's chromaticism and by mysterious LH acc,
where minor broken chords wander far.   LH often
higher than RH.   In Fenesta Vascia, various tonic-
centered cluster chords accompany LH melody twice
through; melody is gradually abandoned by returns to
end piece with pp blend of remote chords hinted at
earlier.   Jaunty Br'er Rabbit uses motive from a
"children's song."   Three-page piece is canonic tour
de force, with canons at the twelfth, double octave,
compound sixth, and fifth.   Lively articulations different in each hand.   Smooth chromaticism in melody of
La Scillitana makes natural the beautiful chromaticism
of chordal acc.   Work grounded on tonic pedal.   Melody of Nolichucky River has many fourths; also fourths
in acc.   Final usual chord with no third (but with
added second, fourth, and lowered sixth) suggests range
of other harmonies.   Sophisticated Spanish atmosphere
in Una Estrella Se Perdidio.   Eight-measure folk music fragment used, but difficult to separate from composer's creation.   Bottled-up excitement released in
final measures with castanet sound.   Direction of
"sternly rhythmic" indicates mood of The Hebrew Children.   For last melody appearances bass harmonization has series of dogged ascending fifths almost oblivious of melody.   Melody omits characteristic second
degree of phrygian mode, but harmony often adds the
tone.   Remaining titles are Gentle Annie, John Ander-
son, My Jo, Bergére Légèr, Jag Unnar Dig Anda Allt
Godt, Goober Peas, Cold Blows the Wind, The Brown

Maid, The Gimcrack, The Reel of Tullochgorum, Sad
Betrayal, Der Butzelmann, My Evaline, Putman's Hill,
A Kansas Cowboy, Incantation, Garufaliá, and Eyes
Dim With Love. (GS, 1965, 45 pp.) 29 pieces. Fngr,
some Ped. 5, some 4.

5.11 BADINGS, HENK. Arcadia VI.
These "easy pieces with thumb under" are truly beautiful, joining austerity and grace. Emotional intensity
reached economically. Lines often have inevitable quality. Five of the works freely use all twelve tones.
Singing tone needed. Legato not always easy. Quite
legible, although "reproduced from the composer's
manuscript." Andante Bicinium (In Two Voices), generates surprising amount of passion. Direction of each
line insistent. Every note is surely important in Epi-
gram. Treble melody, with much dynamic shading,
accompanied by downward moving chromatic thirds.
In Nocturne, garlands of lines unfold, sometimes in as
many as three voices. Centered on D. Boogie-Woogie
attains intensity from characteristic bass (with rotary
motion), from cross accents and slurs against four-beat
motion, and from insistent double note motion. Charming Waltz has swirls of triplets against traditional bass.
Eight-tone symmetrical scale often used, giving final
chord two inflections of third. (Don, 1967, 12 pp.)
9 pieces. MM. 5 & 6, some 4.

5.12 BADINGS, HENK. Vijf Kleine Klavierstukken.
Considerable fantasy and original piano writing in these
beautiful Five Little Piano Pieces. Expressive harmonies are very distantly tonal because of pedal point.
The pp Preludio evokes some mysterious mood. Alternations between lovely chords and melody fragments.
Subtle harmonies, anchored by upper pedal, have tritones. Vivace Strange Writing (4) is scherzo in nature.
Darting LH melody against double note, pedal-like
tremolo. Title may come from differently notated
meters of LH, or from unrelated hands. Moderato
Epilogo has two distinct textures: two legato upper
parts with widely spaced, detached acc or sonorous
melody supported by broken chords. Third piece is
translated Organ Point. (Don, 1967, 9 pp.) MM,
some Ped. 5, 6 & 7.

5.13 BARATI, GEORGE. Rolling Wheels (1956).
An Allegretto scherzando with much use of opening mo-

tive. Two forms of G scale used, each nearly a mirror of the other; much mirror writing in linear contrapuntal texture. Music's logic is compelling. (Mer,
1958, 3 pp.) Fngr, MM. *Anal.

5.14 BAUR, JÜRG. Aphorismen.
Aphorisms are in graceful and effective piano style.
Foreword in German explains that each work is unified
by basic idea, works vary in expressive intention, and
performer may choose his own preference of order.
More music printed on page than usual. Chromatic
tonal harmony is conservative. Andante con moto Old
Dance (I) uses e dorian mode. Phrases of eloquent
treble melody usually begin on strong beats and end
rhythmically weak, often with downward fourth. LH
has legato double note ostinato, and is phrased "to the
end as in the first measure" and "with a little pedal."
Presto agitato Play of the Wind (II) is scherzo in nature. Much rapid hand and finger staccato with both
hands together, and often coupled a fourth apart. Some
syncopation. Spontaneous Witches Dance (IV) is marked
Allegro con fuoco, giocoso, and "always moving."
Skips about with many forearm staccato strokes. Many
key changes. some by sequential motion. Both hands
equally agile. Acc often offbeat parallel fifths. Rec-
ollection (VIII), an expressive Andante, uses one motive repeatedly and imaginatively, usually in polyphonic
texture. Often offbeat parallel fifths or octaves when
LH becomes acc. At double bar, speed "accelerates"
until music is "like the beginning." Allegro molto In
the Character of Til Eulenspiegel (X) scurries brilliantly along with a motive and harmony recalling the
Strauss symphonic poem of same name. Much varied
slurring, wide range, and chromaticism. Translations
are Lament (IV) and "tender," Ostinato (V) and "with
damper pedal," Will of the Wisp (VI), Large Boulders
(VII) and "very sustained and rhythmical" and "broadly,"
Wave Motion (IX), and Lonely Homeward Journey (XI).
(P 14.) (Br&H 6278, 1957, 13 pp.) 12 pieces, 17
min. Fngr, some Ped. 5, 6 & 7.

5.15 BECKWITH, JOHN. The Music Room (1951).
Serious work of beautiful logic. Compositional skill
shown in transitions of first Andantino to Piu allegro
and back again. Compelling contrapuntal lines. Prominent legato double notes, mostly sixths. May be E-
flat or e-flat. No key signature. (In 8.1, 2 pp.)

5.16 BENARY, PETER. Six Miniatures.
Graceful, imaginative. Tonal organization thoroughly
modern, varied and clear. Opportunities for varied
chordal playing. In Bitonal, when RH plays white keys,
LH plays black keys, and vice versa. Beats divided
by two, three, and four. Marked "comfortable." In
Ostinato a quick bass chatter of five tones in varying
order (the ostinato) alternates with twelve-tone set or
cluster chords. Unmetered, played "freely." Lively
Serenade approaches traditional harmony more than
other works of collection, except for Cuckoo. LH has
staccato extended broken triads. Varied rhythms.
Marked "pretty quick." (HG 570, 1967, 6 pp.)

5.17 BENNETT, RICHARD RODNEY. A Week of Birthdays.
These show individuality, naturalness, and integrity.
Fine concern for voice leadings, although texture is
predominantly homophonic. Illustrated verses, beginning with "Monday's child is full of face," indicate pos-
sibility for children but music certainly not childish.
Conservatively new. Monday's Child has fine melodic
line. Mildly chromatic harmonies include tertian,
quartal, and added-note chords. Wednesday's Child
is serious and ingeniously integrated with repetitions
or sequences of leading motive, and secondary role for
same motive. Fine legato practice, including double
notes in LH. Friday's Child, "loving and giving," is
good practice for tone quality, and for legato fourths
and sixths in each hand. (Mil-L 780, 1961, 8 pp.)
7 pieces, 8 min. Fngr, MM, some Ped.

5.18 BERGER, ARTHUR. Intermezzo (1948).
Very American music, with both energy and tenderness.
A Poco andante, marked "with gentleness and expression." Rhythms vitalized by syncopations and endings
of fragments between beats. Melodies have leaps. In
two equal voices, with imitation important. (In 4.1,
2 pp.) MM. Biog.

5.19 BERNAL, MIGUEL. Pastels (1957).
Mexican folk elements attractively shown. Usually conservative, although a few modernisms like polyharmonies and rhythmic displacements. Titles also in Spanish. Moods of Night economically portrayed. Swaying
ostinato of two chords. Flutelike improvisatory melody
uses beats divided by two, three, four and even ten.
Reveille announces dawn in polyharmony. Folk Dance

charms with popular folk elements. In ABA form:
A has rapid LH chromatic acc, using rotary motion;
B volatile with singing sixths and scherzando flights.
Lento <u>Beggars</u> evokes sultry mood with lyrical melody
and ostinato acc or RH repeated octaves starting rapidly and gradually slowing. Well-titled <u>Fiesta</u> has
raucous atmosphere from RH and LH similar fast
speeds, with LH acc using trill-like rotary motion.
Popular sounds emerge from the cacophony of polytonality. (Peer, 1957, 18 pp.) 8 pieces. MM. 5 &
6.

5.20 BERRY, WALLACE. <u>Eight Twentieth-Century Minia-
        tures</u> (1957).
        Fastidious gems with elegant appeal. Popular touches
        sometimes in this sophisticated music. Many could
        serve as a touchstone for contemporary neo-classic
        writing at this level of difficulty. Wide ranges judi-
        ciously used for fuller sound. <u>Waltz,</u> in d phrygian,
        uses subtle waltz rhythm. Mostly two-part writing
        with nearly equal emphasis on each hand. <u>Habanera</u>
        has amazing harmonic and rhythmic sophistication with
        few notes. Long pedals frequently include single high
        or low tones in blend. Rhythm includes triplets across
        two beats. <u>Ostinato,</u> slow, soft, and original, uses
        phrygian mode on a, its only accidental b-natural.
        <u>March,</u> brittle in its brightness, uses quick key shifts,
        neatly placed dissonances, wide keyboard range, and
        forearm staccato or accented touch. (CF, 1967, 12
        pp.) MM, Ped. 5, some 4.

5.21 BLACHER, BORIS. <u>Sonate,</u> Op. 39.
        Fertile wit and appealing charm disguise scrupulous
        organization. Spontaneous rhythm. Graduated variable
        meters progress systematically from two, through three,
        and as far as nine eighth notes in a measure. Simple
        traditional forms. Thin textures. Tempos for first
        movement are allegro and andante, and for second,
        andante and vivace. Within each Andante, material be-
        tween hands irregularly inverted. In two Andantes
        same material used. In closing Vivo, hands alternate
        frequently. Legato thirds. (B&B, 1951, 10 pp.) 2
        movements. MM. 5, 6 & 7.

5.22 BRANSON, DAVID. <u>Two Brazilian Dances.</u>
        <u>Saudade</u> and <u>Samba</u> are modest and appealing at first
        hearing. Conservative. Saudade, marked moderato

piangevole ("weeping"), is "hauntingly sad." Subtle
shifts between sections are skillful. Some harmonic
coloring, like cross relations. Rumba rhythms in
Samba come from LH acc slurred in patterns of three
plus three plus two and interludes with alternating hands
in same pattern; lyrical melody typically syncopated.
(Elk, 1968, 4 pp.) MM, some Ped.

5.23 BRESGEN, CESAR. Balkan Impressions, Vol. 1.
Authenticity and rich fantasy heard in settings of folk
songs and dances from Greece, Yugoslavia, and Bul-
garia. "In many of the pieces these melodies appear
in a simple arrangement, but in others they are used
purely as the foundation for a freer form of composition." Titles and foreword in English and German.
Take the Glass has several fascinating exoticisms:
prominence of augmented second in melody and augmented fourth in acc; prominence of dominant pedal
tone, even against tonic in melody; and unusual scale
for melody, like aeolian, but with lowered fifth. Fanciful Allegretto Diamadula (girl's name) has simple five-
tone melody with augmented second which is much ex-
panded in molto capriccioso section. LH acc pattern
of beginning serves as interlude in second section and
becomes main material in closing section. Serbian
Shepherd's Dance is colorful, effective, and inventive.
Virtuosity required for RH varied slurring and fast
non-legato. LH difficult because of unusual staccato
double notes and faster passage involving extensions
and trill-like figure with first and second fingers. The
9/8 meter in Bulgarian Dance I divided by two plus
two plus two plus three. In D and b aeolian, with only three accidentals. Acc is type of drone bass.
"Stress the 1st, 3rd, 5th, 7th and 8th eighths a little."
Slower Bulgarian Dance II serves as middle section of
Bulgarian Dance I. Here, 9/16 meter is divided by
two plus two plus three plus two. Melody varies between harmonic minor, dorian, and phrygian modes.
(Lit/Pet 5967a, 1964, 14 pp.) 11 pieces. Some Fngr,
MM, some Ped. 5 & 6.

5.24 BRISMAN, HESKEL. Souvenirs.
Ideas clearly developed in this refined music. No key
signatures used for tonal numbers. Dissonances are
mild. Many accidentals and some chromatic harmony
bring no sentimental expressiveness to neo-classic numbers. Clear phrases. Texture usually in two or three

voices. Biography in English and Hebrew. III, an
Allegro commodo, is playfully pervaded by five-note
trill motive. Fairly wide keyboard range. Lento e
cantabile V has lovely cellolike melody convincingly
spun out. Acc often syncopated seconds. VI, a bright
sounding Allegretto grazioso, has two ideas, each repeated. Lively articulations and a two-note syncopated slur mark second idea. Free use of chromaticism. Hands equally emphasized. In VII, marked
Adagietto, opening motive used throughout, its tonal
journeys suggested by first two appearances, first in
b (although ending on an eleventh chord on d-sharp),
then in g. Texture fuller than usual, with four-note
chords. (IMI, 1965, 17 pp.) 8 pieces, 9 min.
Fngr. Biog. 5, some 4.

5.25 CALABRO, LOUIS. Diversities.
Contrary charm in these contrasting pieces provided
by tonal harmonies which seem arbitrary but prove
to be consistent, skillful, and even mildly original.
Raga is exotic. Ornate melodic fragment, with acc of
broken chord of two superimposed fifths, each with
added sixth. Pedalling may be a problem. The ppp
Dream is strange and evocative. Many melodic and
harmonic major sevenths; final chord of a fifth, with
staccato lower and upper minor ninths, is typical.
Tones of Chorale have some relationship to e-flat dorian mode. In four parts. Questions has sixths and
thirds with much cross relation. Melodic improvisation in the fast Blues moves "freely" above constant
LH minor sevenths. Air, like Reflection, is utterly
simple. Key may be E, or e, with competition from
E-flat. Petite Sonatine has merry play with cross re-
lations--two on final arpeggiated chord. Attractive
syncopations. (EV, 1967, 16 pp.) 14 pieces. MM,
some Ped. 5, some 4 & 6.

5.26 CALABRO, LOUIS. Suite of Seven.
Thoughtful, with some originality. Freely tonal, its
harmonic density comes from polyharmony, chord
streams moving in contrary motion, and chords moving stepwise. Consistency of a few harmonic intervals
(thirds and sixths) in several pieces. Writing balanced
between chordal and passage work. In the improvisatory Prelude some scale passages wander as to key.
At end C emerges over A-flat tones. Hymn is in four-
part harmony with modal progressions. Several cross

relations. Blues, has two voices with polytonal tend-
ency. (EV, 1964, 7 pp.) MM. 5, some 6.

5.27 CALABRO, LOUIS. Young People's Sonatine.
Attractive introduction to neo-classic music at this
level of difficulty. Conservative harmony. Allegretto
grazioso flows smoothly in consonant two-voice texture.
In A-flat, with harmonic side-slipping, particularly at
cadences, such as b to A-flat chord at end. Lento
assai, played "with warmth," is chordal. A-flat harmonies striking for chords like minor dominants. Has
enharmonic changes. Last movement, marked "smart,
quick," has complex rhythm of changing meters, irregular accents, and rests. LH chords often triads. (EV,
1957, 6 pp.) 3 movements. MM. 5, some 4.

5.28 CARLSTEDT, JAN. Intermezzo (1962).
Marked Mesto, this work has commanding logic.
Coupled melody and harmony, or fuller textured contrary motion. Polyharmonies result from voice leading, usually by seconds. Builds to fff climax. (In
5.5, 1 p.)

5.29 CASADESUS, ROBERT. Six Enfantines, Op. 48.
Admirable musical unity and piano writing in Six Pieces
for Children. Fine variety includes two humorous
pieces. Titles make these primarily for children.
Some octave reaches. Barcarolle has piquant harmonic
charm, deftly introducing polychords. Some RH arpeggios. Directions are "lean on LH" and "more and
more gentle." Renard (i.e. Fox) From Spain is subtle
and sly: ostinato bass emphasizes subdominant, turn-
ing to tonic only at end. Fine RH finger staccato
study, describing "Spanish chickens." Gentle and lyrical Legend on the Name of Charlie Chaplin uses motto
based on the spelling of Chaplin, pretending white keys
continue the alphabet after g, and indicated in the
score. Melody in RH weaker fingers, stronger fingers
used for some acc. (Dur, 1955, 12 pp.) MM, Ped.
Ch. 5, some 4.

5.30 CASTELNUOVO-TEDESCO, MARIO. Prelude.
Neo-romantic "semplice e tranquillo." Concise lyrical
material has two voices (much imitation) filled out
some by chords. Splendid for arm use in singing
touch. Striking ending with lush seventh chords, appoggiaturas, and coupled chords. Tonal, with free use

of all twelve tones. (In 4.1, 3 pp.) Fngr, some Ped. Biog.

5.31 CHAILLY, LUCIANO. Due Istantanee (1950 & 1954).
Two Snapshots are lovely. Directions like "immater-
ial" and "vague" suggest impressionist nature. Tempos
slow. Mostly middle upper register. Broadly tonal;
one twelve-tone set used most poetically near end of
second number. Epigraph for Daniela paraphrases
from Romans: "Death has no power beyond death, but
what is alive, is because of God." First Words of
Ricardo paraphrases Luke: "His mouth was opened
and he was able to speak." Builds to climax with ac-
celerating ostinato and dotted note octaves. (Ric,
1956, 2 pp.) MM, some Ped.

5.32 CONSTANTINIDIS, YANNIS. Greek Miniatures, Vol 2
(1948-51).
High musical and pianistic quality of first volume (see
3.18) continues. Often four voices with melody sometimes in inner part. Acc may be rhythmically counter
to melody as notated, and, in general, is more independent of melody than in first volume. Form of XIX
is AABB and coda. Acc varies between three added
voices and broken chords. For its four-voice setting,
XXI requires legato fingering, including changing fingering on held tones. Trills and grace notes decorate
melody. For fuller setting in XXII, LH holds every
other half-beat tone in rhythm contrary to melody
rhythm. Many ornaments in the exotic XXIV. Melody
has chromatic changes and augmented seconds. In
7/8. Melody of XXX confined to two two-measure
phrases using only four or five different tones. Each
pattern set three different ways, one complicated by
overlapping tones. (Ron, 1951 & 1957, 14 pp.) 14
pieces, 10 min, 30 sec. Fngr, MM, Ped. 5, some
4 & 6.

5.33 COWELL, HENRY. Toccatina.
Vivace. Lively spirit of hoe down. In first section
LH has fast sixteenth notes while RH acc has offbeat
four-note chords. Role of hands reversed in middle
section. Fine dynamic variety. (In 4.1, 1 p.) Fngr.
Biog.

5.34 DAHL, INGOLF. First March.
Swaggering and tuneful Allegro. Tonal. Fine variety

between legato and staccato. Equal distribution between hands. In "miniature Sonata-Allegro form."
May be grouped with 5.35 and 5.36 to "form a Sonatina alla marcia." (Pr, 1957, 2 pp.) Fngr. *Anal.

5.35 DAHL, INGOLF. Second March.
Stately funeral march. Uses traditional materials with
mild innovations, such as ending with low fourth to ce-
ment tonic chord without third. Wide spacing between
hands. Has polyphonic interest. Dotted rhythms suggest "a slowly measured tread" of honest grief. (Pr,
1957, 2 pp.) Fngr. *Anal.

5.36 DAHL, INGOLF. Third March (1956).
"Jolly music" has irresistible spontaneity. Hints of
commonplace tunefulness without being hackneyed. In
an Allegro 6/8. (Pr, 1957, 2 pp.) Fngr. *Anal.

5.37 DAMASE, JEAN-MICHEL. Pastorale.
Fascinating work! Wide-spaced melody has sevenths
and ninths, and acc has harmonic seconds and sevenths:
total effect is melodious and piquantly consonant. Only
white keys. Ninth reach. (In 3.6, 2 pp.)

5.38 DEFOSSEZ, RENÉ. Les Caprices de Ma Poupée
     (1950).
Brightly imaginative music depicts titles of The Caprices of My Doll. Clever modulations within solid
tonality, piquant higher pitch dissonances, and high
ranges in general combine to give pieces attractive
but prudent modernities. Five fast pieces. Keys
range through two flats and four sharps. Shuttle-Cock
(p 4) is amusing novelty. Many offbeat staccato seconds, sevenths, or ninths, as well as grace notes leap-
ing an octave. Dynamic shifts add humor. Lullaby
(p 9), based on tonic pedals, uses mild dissonances
for gentle coloring. RH legato double notes and LH
extended broken chords. Le Diabolo (game with a
spinning top) scurries up the keyboard hand over hand
by measured trills, increasing volume into dissonant
broken chords; then down the keyboard with softening
chromatic major ninth chords. Sudden dynamic changes
add to playful spirit. Translations are The Piano Les-
son (p 2), My Doll Plays at Being a Soldier (p 6), and
Dance on the Chord (p 10). (SF, 1960 & 1966, 14 pp.)
6 pieces. Fngr. MM, some Ped. Ch. 5, some 4 &
6.

5.39 DELL'ANNO, LEANDER. Three Short Piano Pieces.
Combines tension and relaxation, typical of jazz. Lament is based on freely altered ostinato pattern;
rhythm includes short-longs and triplets. Mostly in
two-part texture. Back Talk is snappy with staccatos,
short rests, syncopations, and accents. (MJQ, 1963,
4 pp.) Fngr, MM. 5 & 6.

5.40 DELLO JOIO, NORMAN. Night Song.
Delicate and evocative Lento. Two minor triads and
two major triads, each pair a tritone apart and usually juxtaposed, are used imaginatively; both polyharmony and tonality result. Ranges are wide. Melody,
like arabesque, has sound of Oriental flute. (In 4.1,
2 pp.) Fngr, some Ped. Biog.

5.41 DENISOV, A. Bagatelles, Op. 19 (1960).
Frequently appealing near-novelty numbers have unusual harmonic twists. Scherzando element in four works.
Traditional piano writing includes rapid hand staccatos.
A few meter signature changes. Allegretto I has harmonies like dominant chord with double inflection of
third and raised fifth. Interestingly gauche Andantino
III has LH quintuplet perpetual motion acc, good thumb
study. Melody includes triplets. RH patter in VII
has naive quality. RH has many sevenths, etc, using
hand staccato. Some polychords. Translation of in-
sert on page 14 is "correction of misprints" and refers first to "page 2, line 7, measure 2." Correction
printed in last column. (IV, V.) (Sov, 1963, 14
pp.) 7 pieces. Fngr, MM, Ped. 5 & 6.

5.42 DRAKEFORD, RICHARD. Six Transatlantic Studies
(1961).
Irresistible spin-off from jazz with economical means.
Delightfully witty quick mood shifts, harmonic surprises, and rhythmic quirks. Serious art. Usually
fast. For the Prelude: The Blue Moon, composer's
directions of "moderately fast, cool, and steady,"
"melodiously," "roughly," "bittersweet," "cheerfully,"
and "mind!" are just right. Weekend Rag has ground
bass moving from tonic to dominant through raised
fourth. Triple measures interrupt. Effective harmonic minor seconds. Very fast Greased Lightning has
lively rhythm from irregular slurrings, accents, and
meter changes. Clashes of simultaneous cross relations, usually on blues notes. (Elk/Galx, 1967, 8

pp.) 5, some 6.

5.43 DRIESSLER, JOHANNES. Drei Sonatinen, Op. 29/2.
Most reliable craftsmanship in Three Sonatinas. Each
is in three movements, middle movements beginning
with specified German folk song. Very German nature
of the works (sound like Hindemith) emerges from medieval sounds of fourths and fifths, form clarity, and
predominance of polyphony, usually non-imitative. Tonal harmonies use all twelve tones moderately. Lively
rhythmic interest. Music falls naturally under the
hands, and depends mostly on finger legato and staccato. Moderate ranges. Difficulty increases moderately with each work. In Sonatina III, meter varies
between 2/4 and 3/4 in the pleasant Allegretto. RH
has many chords of two fourths. Hand staccato.
Adagio is much like fifteenth-century German lied with
dorian and aeolian influences, partial imitation and legato three or four-voice writing. Many fifths. Allegro molto has three types of texture: two voices artic-
ulated diversely in 12/8 meter, molto legato three and
four voices in 3/4 meter, and fanciful one-line broken
chord play. (Bär 2694, 1955, 21 pp.) Each about 7
min. MM. 5 & 6, some 4.

5.44 FARKAS, FERENC. Three Initials (1962).
Splendidly accessible studies in two (rarely three) part
imitative counterpoint. Titles also in Hungarian and
German. Twelve-tone music, with some accommoda-
tion to tonality, particularly in II, its subject having
tonal intervals of fifth and fourths. II has subject in
diminution; III has invertible counterpoint. (EMB,
1967, 6 pp.)

5.45 FLOYD, CARLISLE. Episodes, Vol. II.
Music of character and individuality. Differences from
Vol. 1 (see 4.48) include: (a) wider key range, (b)
frequent dotted rhythms (one work uses 6/4 meter),
and (c) versions of melody/acc texture. Fanfare,
marked Allegro ben ritmico, has rhythmic patter of
two rapid repeated tones; hands often have pattern together and are frequently a second apart. In two
voices. Processional gains martial and unified character from acc single-note rhythm of long and two
shorts (or reverse) and accented RH short-long rhythm
of legato thirds and triads. Thirds are dissonant.
Allegro Jig is "robusto" from added-note percussive

harmonies. Frequent modulations. Short-short-long
rhythms. In Night Song two lovely voices move in
same rhythm, often in contrary motion, in medium upper range. During held melody tones, added-note
chords fill in lower register. Contented mood of Andante moderato Morning Song comes from cantabile
melody and swaying acc of legato thirds. Hands alternate. Some mixolydian C mode. Allegro Dance is optimistic and attractive. Unusual in collection for sections with no modulation; first and last sections are
solely in A lydian mode. Uses agile fingers in both
hands. (B&H, 1965, 21 pp.) 12 pieces. Fngr, MM,
some Ped. 5 & 6, some 4.

5.46 FRANK, MARCEL G. Bagatelle.
Bright and entertaining. Varied articulations and dynamics. Hand staccatos. Much ostinato. In f, with
chords and melodies using fourths. MM marking seems
slow. (MCA, 1967, 2 pp.) MM.

5.47 FRANKELL, MANUEL. The Three Days Piano Sona-
     tina.
Clever work of immediate appeal, no pretensions.
Very tonal harmonies take unexpected turns. Suave and
graceful melodies. Basic neo-classic impression includes full presence of sentiment. Happy Days in regular first movement Sonatina form. Key is certainly
G, but music is soon in B-flat. Melody of second
theme, after an early drop of major seventh, proceeds
with no more surprises. Thin texture usually filled out
by thirds and sixths. Crisp and varied articulation.
Andantino Lazy Days luxuriates in Poco animato section with typical romantic fullness; builds to con fuoco
climax. Cliches galore in jolly Holidays: syncopations,
added-note chords, suggestions of boogie bass, irresistible march tune, ninth chords, blues harmonies--
all good-naturedly pass in review. Conservative. (Hin/
Pet 1435, 1959, 14 pp.) 3 movements, 9 min. Fngr,
MM, some Ped.

5.48 GALLOIS-MONTBRUN, RAYMOND. March of the Ghosts.
Smartly stylish tonal writing. These ghosts aren't very
frightening. Pleasant enharmonic progressions and other mild harmonic surprises. Useful for wandering
among sharps and flats. RH has dotted note melody using quick extensions. (In 5.1, 2 pp.) Some Fngr, MM,
some Ped. Ch.

5.49 GENZMER, HARALD. Pièce Brève.
Short Piece has fine musical play. A neo-classic
Giocoso poco. In two voices, with LH acc using extensions like major seventh between fifth and second
finger. Shifts between 4/4 and 6/8; also simultaneous 6/8 and 3/4. (In 5.2, 2 pp.) Fngr. Biog.

5.50 GEORGE, EARL. Banjo Serenade.
Extrovert fun, reminiscent of minstrel show. Middle
section imitates a continual strumming with its perpetual motion and bitonality. First section has poly-
rhythm, because LH has ostinato of six eighth notes
while RH melody is in simple 4/4. Needs hand independence. (Oxf, 1960, 4 pp.) Fngr, MM.

5.51 GREEN, RAY. Short Sonata in F.
Appealing directness, solidly based in American jazz,
folk, and hymn idioms. Refreshing, unified, and uncomplicated. Opening and Ending Movements similar.
Traditional sonata form. Very tonal contrary motion
harmonies, with added diatonic tones (RH may have
fourth chords), alternate with coupled writing, usually
two but sometimes as many as six octaves apart.
Small-step melodies and many syncopations amid
duple rhythms. Second slower-motion themes change
to triple rhythm and may have cross relationship.
Melody in Pastorale may include different inflections
of chord tone. LH broken chords, with added sixth,
often move by thirds. Chorale always has two fourths
in RH and one third in LH. (AME, 1951 & 1964, 10
pp.) 4 movements, 6 min, 45 sec. MM. 5 & 6.

5.52 GUARNIERI, M. CAMARGO. Suite Mirim.
Little Suite has South American flavor. Usually tonal.
Technically consistent, with opportunity for legato
practice. A Popular Song (III) is reflective Andante.
In three voices, with lower two often imitating leading
voice. Fine for legato touch and singing tone. Children's Game (IV) has bold folklike melody in lydian
and mixolydian modes. Hands alternate. Acc of rapid broken fourths (no black keys) creates different colored sheen from tune. Translations (when known) are
"without hurrying" (I), and Small Tango (II). (Ric-Ba,
1955, 7 pp.) 4 pieces. MM. 5, some 6 & 7.

5.53 HAIEFF, ALEXEI. Four Juke Box Pieces.
Familiar and banal echoes emerge now and then from

sophisticated harmonies, as title suggests. Works
call for effective interpretations. Recalls music of
Poulenc or Prokofieff. Accessible March has sudden
accents, some polyharmony, varied articulations,
staccato broken tenths, and some legato and staccato
octaves. Expressive factors in bewitching Nocturne
are varied repetitions and much rhythmic variety, including syncopation. Relaxed atmosphere from triplet-
oriented RH melody and broken chord acc. In F-
sharp (no key signature), with many cadences in g.
Waltz may be played with a cornet obbligato. (B&H,
1952, 11 pp.) Some Ped. 5 & 6.

5.54 HAJDU, MIHÁLY. Footrace.
Delightful extrovert Vivace. Useful technically for
rotary motion and for fast repeated tones in LH. In
two voices, except for frequent additions of accented
harmonic minor seconds. (In 4.8, 1-1/2 pp.) Fngr.

5.55 HARSANYI, TIBOR. Etude.
Ingenious perpetual motion Presto. Merry single-note
modal melody, interrupted by slurred double notes, is
accompanied by rapid LH repeated tones. Acc shifts
to accommodate final phrase tone, or itself is final
tone, and then music is off again in new color. Hands
equal in agility. (In 5.2, 2 pp.) Fngr. Biog.

5.56 HARTIG, HEINZ FRIEDRICH. Little Sonata, Op. 27
      (1957).
Distinction and originality results from masterly new
assembly of the old. Classic temperament. Tonal,
using all twelve tones freely; also includes seventh and
fourth chords. Measure awareness necessary in
rhythms of Allegro. 6/8 meter has noticeable rests
and shifts to 3/4. Melody varied in thoughtful Andante; acc consists of broken thirteenth chords on two
staves. Allegro molto vivace accented irregularly.
Light texture includes repeated chords. Returns to
material of first movement. (B&B, 1958, 6 pp.) 3
movements.

5.57 HARVEY, PAUL. Rumba Toccata.
Musically simple and appealing Presto agitato, con ritmo. Amid perpetual sixteenth note motion, LH pecks
out tones grouped by three plus three plus two to form
melody. RH alternating acc has repeated single tones
or octaves. Conservative. (Ric-L, 1961, 2 pp.)

55 sec. Fngr, MM.

5.58 HEDGES, ANTHONY. Scherzetto.
Busy Vivace of neo-classic clarity. Easy to interpret.
Tonal, with all twelve tones used. Harmonic progressions by movement up or down a step. Much melodic
motion by fourths and fifths. Variety of articulations,
with opportunity for forearm staccato. Equal hand facility. (Ric-L, 1964, 3 pp.) 1 min, 20 sec. Fngr,
MM.

5.59 HELPS, ROBERT. Starscape.
Most delicate and awesome. Detailed dynamics, usually from p to ppp, with much pedal blend for varied
treble ranges and few bass tones. Harmony, both
clear and clouded, is centered on A with definite cadence and has color play between G-sharp and G-natural; brief passage of near-tone row with change of texture. (In 4.1, 2 pp.) MM, Ped. Biog.

5.60 HODDINOTT, ALUN. Sonatina, Op. 18.
Effective neo-classic work, with sophisticated workmanship. Freely tonal, with much chromaticism.
Often coupled writing. Prelude is rhythmically fanciful. Measures often begin with rest or tied note; also
varied number of thirty-second notes used during quarter note beat. Facile Scherzo often one-line music
which spreads out or in by contrary motion. Has trem-
olos and trills. Remote and deeply emotional Elegy
moves by small steps. In Presto Finale, irregularly
slurred line has many seconds and fourths, although intervals usually are unpredictable. Each movement
moves attacca to next. Written for piano or clavichord.
(St&B, 1964, 10 pp.) 4 movements. 5, 6 & 7.

5.61 HOLD, TREVOR. Fun With Twelve Notes, Op. 4.
Elegant and sophisticated writing. Valuable for individual harmonies; tonal, but one tone of a triad may be
perversely changed or there may be polyharmonies.
Other musical elements traditional. Fast Prelude is
to be played "with humour." Sounds like a nursery
tune with polyharmonies. Straightforward rhythms.
Exquisite and lyric Waltz I is in C, with all twelve
tones freely used; ends with tonic eleventh. Thirds
and sixths in acc. Melody hands reversed for second
half. Reel rolls happily along hand over hand whether
in G or g, whether lowering the second and fifth de-

grees or not.   The genuine S̲a̲d̲ ̲S̲o̲n̲g̲ has LH acc of
thirds and sixths to help foc̲u̲s̲ ̲h̲a̲r̲m̲o̲n̲y̲.   (St&B, 1966,
15 pp.) 10 pieces.   MM.   5, some 4.

5. 62 HÖLLER, KARL.   S̲o̲n̲a̲t̲i̲n̲e̲ ̲I̲, Op. 58, No. 1.
Bright optimism and wholesome unpretentiousness characterize this fine melodic work.   Modernisms are not
troubling.   Neo-classic.   Tonal, freely using all twelve
tones.` Fine dynamic variety.   Allegro moderato
shows unity.   Interesting key shifts.   Acc of rhythmic
distinction.   Scherzando enlivened by capricious triads
with register contrast.   Equal hand emphasis.   III, a
Poco lento, is lovely pastel.   Acc uses gentle major
seconds and other color chords.   IV is a rondo marked
Vivo e leggiero.   Four different sevenths, as well as
eleventh and thirteenth chords, accompany a rapid five-
finger passage.   Chromaticisms bring piquant harmonies.   (ScS 4817, 1963, 10 pp.)   4 movements.
Some Ped.

5. 63 HOVLAND, EGIL.   R̲o̲n̲d̲i̲n̲o̲, Op. 29, No. 2.
Clever and facile.   Stark sounds of high range, single-
note melody with parallel thirdless harmonies.   Harmonies include bitonality and added-note chords.
Rhythmically challenging.   Coupled, or even quadrupled
writing.   (Ly 370, 1958, 3 pp.)   MM.

5. 64 JAQUE, RHENÉ.   M̲i̲s̲c̲h̲i̲e̲f̲.
Spontaneous and delightful.   Title borne out by quick
shifts between brusque, tumbling staccato fifths and
lyrical small-interval treble melody; sudden dynamic
shifts also.   Tonal harmony freely uses all twelve
tones.   (GVT, 1968, 2 pp.)   MM.

5. 65 JAQUE, RHENÉ.   T̲w̲o̲ ̲T̲w̲o̲-̲P̲a̲r̲t̲ ̲I̲n̲v̲e̲n̲t̲i̲o̲n̲s̲.
Effective and well-integrated.   In synthetic modes, intervals like augmented seconds and tritones easily in-
corporated.   Deeply subjective Andante starts with
imitation, then subject is abandoned for short develop-
ments of a motive, with important sequence.   Rollicking Allegro uses scalelike subject more; inversion included.   In both numbers, particularly second, an independent voice becomes acc for brief periods.   (BMI,
1963, 4 pp.)   Some MM.   5 & 6.

5. 66 JÁRDÁNYI, PÁL.   S̲o̲n̲a̲t̲i̲n̲a̲, No. 2.
Purity and simplicity combined in work of splendid in-

tegrity. Secure and economical craftsmanship. Pleasant Andantino, in g aeolian mode, has texture of RH
melody and LH acc. LH frequently has fifth finger
held, with slow trill for first and second. Jaunty,
molto marcato Allegro (a rondo), is often in G mixolydian mode. RH melody uses forearm staccato. LH
has fifth finger held, with other fingers in detached
scale pattern. Color contrast comes in each movement in shift from seven-tone mode to pentatonic mode.
(In 4.10, 5 pp.) 2 movements. MM.

5.67 KARKOFF, MAURICE. Miniatyrsvit, Op. 39 (1958-
   59).
   Works in Miniature Suite are harmonically searching,
   broadly tonal, and strongly influenced by voice leading,
   with noticeable contrary motion. Chords with double
   inflections and polychords. More music than usual on
   printed page. Two slow and two fast numbers. Small
   Sad Prelude (1), an Andante mesto of haunting expressiveness, is in two, three, and four voices. Legato
   double notes in each hand. Intermezzo I is whimsical
   Allegro with distinct alternation between leggiero pp
   passages and f, irregularly accented three-note dissonant chords. Trill-like, leggiero passages move either
   in contrary or parallel motion. (Geh, 1960, 6 pp.)
   4 pieces. Fngr, MM, Ped. 5 & 6.

5.68 KENINS, T. Rondino.
   Jolly Allegretto, traditional except for chromatic shifts.
   For first such surprise, after D is established, Neapolitan root position chord heard without warning. Each
   hand has rapid five-finger runs and some fast scales.
   LH has forearm staccatos. Fairly wide range. Conservative. (GVT, 2 pp--also in 4.11.) MM.

5.69 KERR, HARRISON. Frontier Day.
   Extrovert Scherzando. Of neo-classic temperament.
   "... strong polytonal characteristics." Splendid practice in forearm rotation and flexible hand positions on
   black keys. Expressive slower middle section has legato RH double notes. (Mer, 1958, 3 pp.) *Anal.
   Fngr, MM.

5.70 KHACHATURIAN, ARAM. Sonatina (1959).
   Effective, and musically simple. Tonal, with colorful
   modulations. Homophonic with many sequences.
   Rhythm has some irregularity. Merry and fluent Al-

legro giocoso includes obvious first theme and chromatic cantabile middle section.   LH has staccato,
medium fast broken and unbroken octaves.   Andante
con anima, rubato has graceful flow.   Some sensitive
harmonies.   LH has much legato double note acc, particularly sixths.   Allegro mosso has facile play with
familiar harmonies.   Smooth shifts from metric patterns to irregular passages, with eighth note constant.
Sounds more difficult than it is.   (Leeds-NY, 1964,
21 pp.) Fngr, MM, Ped.   5, 6 & 7.

5.71 KIRCHNER, LEON.   Little Suite.
Fascinating security amid variety.   Shows complex
musical thinking which is, happily, communicated.
Lyrical line always apparent.   In each movement repeated tone or chord usually indicates tonality; otherwise, much harmonic freedom.   Meters often change.
Allegretto Toccata must be mastered to be appreci-
ated.   Rhythmically irregular, distinct strand of melody binds whole together.   Neighboring staccato tones
often form acc.   Ending of E-flats held against staccato Ds gives hint of tonal freedom.   In the passionate
Adagio Fantasy, sforzando e minor chords are anchor
for rhapsodic coupled melody.   (Merc, 1950, 5 pp.)
5 movements.   MM.   5 & 6.

5.72 KOCH, ERLAND Von.   Lyrisk Scen (1962).
Lyric Scene takes full advantage of piano's low range
to create full texture.   Melodically attractive and
simple.   Much motivic writing, some coupled.   Motive inverted on second page.   Fine climaxes of contrary motion triads--result is polyharmony.   In b-flat.
(In 5.5, 2 pp.) MM, Ped.

5.73 KOHS, ELLIS B.   Scherzo.
Energetic, extrovert, and convincing.   Irregular
rhythms alternating between 2/2 and 3/4.   Percussive
harmonies, with added seconds or fourths.   Lydian influence.   Forearm staccato requires subdued thumb.
(Mer, 1958, 2 pp.) Fngr, MM.   *Anal.

5.74 KRAFT, LEO.   Perky Pete.
Irresistible spirit.   Flexible composition techniques
with dissonances and many fourths easily absorbed.
Has rapid repeated tones.   Syncopations and meter
changes assure lively rhythm.   (In 4.2, 2 pp.)
*Anal.

5.75 KUNC, BOZIDAR. The Favourite Fairy Tale.
Like a salon piece. Fine study in sonority is marked
Molto moderato con dolcezza, with quite full texture
(much pedal), but "delicato." Parallel stepwise chords
in treble, while bass retains same harmony with slow
trill. Harmony has chromatic coloring. Neo-romantic and conservative. (In 4.12, 3 pp.) Fngr, MM,
Ped. *Biog.

5.76 LA MONTAINE, JOHN. A Child's Picture Book, Op.
7.
Works of decided character. Strong tonal harmonic
profile, with free use of all twelve tones. Chordal
textures predominate. Some octaves. In The Giant
Has a Hobby-Horse, full arm ff strokes used "with a
big swing" in both hands on single tones and chords.
In a, but triads wander. Pedal may be troublesome.
Story for a Rainy Day, marked tenderly, uses singing
touch on single tones and octaves in lovely quiet mood.
Fine legato double note and pedal study. Jack Frost
depicted with crisp staccato upper ranges and sforzandos. Imaginative, with much dynamic variety.
Polyharmony hints. Usually one line music, hands
alternating. (BrB, 1957, 10 pp.) 5 pieces. 5 min,
55 sec. MM, Ped. Ch. 5, some 6 & 7.

5.77 LAVAGNE, ANDRÉ. What Time Is It?
Familiar tones of Westminster's Big Ben in parallel
major sixths (involving cross relation) and clanging
dissonant strokes. Some three-tone legato chords without pedal. In E. (In 3.6, 2 pp.) MM, Ped.

5.78 LESSARD, JOHN. Little Concert.
Shows exquisite craftsmanship. Expressive purposes
apparent when care is taken with many interesting details. Stravinsky and Copland influences. Often tenderly lyrical. Tonal, with sparse use of accidentals.
Very careful editing, especially pedaling. Accessible
Dance, in ABA form, has well-contrasted sections.
In A, irregular length melody phrases often begin after
a rest. B built over ostinato of two chords. Lullaby
gently appealing. Faster section has flexible rhythm
and articulation. Pandiatonic harmonies at beginning
and end; clearly tonal at main cadences. Much attractive articulation detail in Allegretto Procession. Resourceful textures, with irregular pedaling. (Jos,
1964, 15 pp.) 6 movements. MM, Ped. 5, some 4.

5.79 LESUR, DANIEL. L'Armoricaine.
      Cantabile Woman from Brittany tastefully set, with in-
      itial dependence on fingers alone and fuller setting with
      pedal later. Often coupled writing. Legato repeated
      tones. Modal influences in melody. Free materials of
      appropriate character used between appearance of folk
      melody. (In 8.2, 2 pp.) Fngr, some Ped.

5.80 LESUR, DANIEL. Heart-Ache (1950).
      Deeply probing, sophisticated music. In a, with last
      broken chord of A, B, g-sharp, g^1 and e^2 indicating
      wide explorations. Splendid opportunity for cultivating
      arm weight. Fine texture variety. RH acc often has
      legato double notes. (In 3.6, 1 p.) Fngr, MM.

5.81 LHOTKA-KALINSKI, IVO. Microforms.
      Fragments of bird songs, headed by words of Paul
      Dukas: "Listen to the birds, they are great masters."
      Music is twelve-tone, combined "with an introverted
      impressionistic style." Counting necessary. More
      contemporary than other numbers in collection. (In
      4.12, 2 pp.) 4 pieces. MM. *Biog.

5.82 LIDHOLM, INGVAR. Sonatin (1947).
      Fresh twists to familiar materials in two-voice tex-
      ture. In g. Neo-classic and convincing. Opening
      Marsch swaggers gracefully with dotted rhythms and
      mildly angular melody. Pastoral is simple and lovely.
      In treble register, with piquant chromatic coloring in
      LH acc. Like other movements, Rondo is musically
      transparent. High spirits denoted by staccatos and ac-
      cents, but middle section more reserved. Frequent
      meter changes. (In 6.6, 3 pp.) 3 movements. MM.
      Biog. 5, some 4.

5.83 LILJEFORS, INGEMAR. Bagatell (1962).
      Mood is quiet and consistent. Diatonic, with some
      evidence of polytonality. Progressions always by small
      steps. Excellent opportunity for practising tone quality
      and legato double notes in each hand. (In 5.5, 1 p.)

5.84 LINDE, BO. Hymn (1962).
      Granite integrity and severity mark this work, remind-
      ing one of medieval organum, although there is a main
      melody. Melody harmonized at times by parallel
      fourth, first inversion or seventh chords. Has inter-
      locking scales and harmonic sixths. (In 5.5, 2 pp.)

5.85 LLOYD, NORMAN. Five Pieces for Dance (1935,
        1937, 1939.)
      Subtle transformations of popular musical elements,
      suggested by titles like Puritan Hymn and Blues,
      pervade these works. Always inherently musical.
      First conceived to go with contemporary dance. Thor-
      oughly contemporary tonal harmonies, including many
      fourths and double inflections. For Dance Hall Study,
      out-of-tune piano indicated by high range chromatic
      fourths in flexible rhythms. Tonic and dominant bass
      alternates with added note chords of much harmonic
      interest. Theme and Variations has abstract mood
      set by main angular melody. Considerable fantasy
      in the five Variations. Wide keyboard range and var-
      ied piano techniques convincingly used. (Orc, 1963,
      12 pp.) Some MM & Ped. 5, some 4.

5.86 LOPATNIKOFF, NIKOLAI. Dance Piece.
      "Gay, lilting" Allegro grazioso. Decidedly neo-classic.
      Meters change frequently amid constant motion. Mild-
      ly dissonant percussive harmonies add to rhythmic bite,
      as well as varied articulations. In A-flat. Many
      staccatos and slightly extended leaps make excellent
      keyboard-acquaintance study. (Pr, 1956, 4 pp.) MM.
      *Anal.

5.87 McBRIDE, ROBERT. School Bus (Stop).
      Good-natured. Harmonies are obviously those of C;
      however, out-of-key chords as well as modulations add
      spice. Excellent for forearm rotation on broken oc-
      taves and the like. (In 4.2, 2 pp.) Fngr, MM, some
      Ped. *Anal.

5.88 MACONCHY, ELIZABETH. The Yaffle.
      Yaffle is a green woodpecker, musically treated with
      superior imagination, Allegro vigoroso, e ritmico.
      Based in G, with alluring middle section in mixolydian
      mode. Hands alternate some. In 5/4. (Ric-L, 1961,
      3 pp.) 1 min, 30 sec. Fngr, Ped.

5.89 MANEN, CHRISTIAN. Arabesques.
      Obvious music with attractive, exotic folk elements,
      apparently authentic from North Africa. Two works
      use drone acc patterns. Melodies, always in treble,
      often have traditional augmented seconds and other
      chromaticism. Sunsets in the Mahoura (up-country)
      (II) has fanciful treble melody. One-measure ostinato

acc with repeated thumb tones. In the Desert (III) is
in Hungarian minor scale. Melody often doubled by
LH in octaves, fourths, or fifths. Directions indicate
"elephants and camels" for acc and "the Arab's song"
for melody. I is translated The Markets of Biskra.
(Bil, 1968, 7 pp.) 3 pieces. MM. 5, some 6.

5.90 MARTIN, FRANK. Clair de lune.
Undemonstrative Moonlight well subtitled A Little Nocturne. Both melody and acc have much chromatic motion in C. Treble melody moves usually by small
step. Ostinatolike acc progresses constantly by sixteenths; it has moderate extensions. (In 5.2, 2 pp.)
MM. Biog.

5.91 MARTINŮ, BOHUSLAV. A Composition for Little
      Elves.
Gay composition useful for chromaticism in tonal music. Rapid legato and staccato sixteenths, usually for
RH. LH has many slower double notes. Conservative. (In 4.7, 2 pp.) *Biog. Ch.

5.92 MATYS, JIŘÍ. Obrázky ze Zimy, Op. 36 (1963).
Winter Pictures have natural, gentle charm. Splendid
for children, yet refreshing naiveté for all ages. Traditional forms and keyboard writing. Appealing harmonies pose few problems. Tonal or modal, no key
signatures, many sharps. Numerous two and three-
tone chords; a few octaves. Much treble range. Insti-
gated by, and dedicated to Moravian teachers. Biography and titles in Czech. Harmonies for Snow Is
Falling (1) are predominately pastel. Has melodic
sevenths. Some material reversed between hands. In
B, although beginning has a G triad, and tonic ending
with an added fourth and sixth, as well as lowered
fifth. White Night (5) is lovely. Dorian mode on f-
sharp, as well as fourths and fifths, suggest ancient
times. Jingle of Sleigh Bells (6) comes from Presto
assai hand alternation in treble register. Many harmonic fourths; leading RH has only fourths and fifths.
Usually pp. Translations are Snow Ball Fight (2), On
the Sled (3), A Short Carol (4), and We Like Winter
(7). (Pan, 1965, 13 pp.) 7 pieces. MM, Ped. Biog.
5, some 4.

5.93 MEYEROWITZ, JAN. Noel Far from Home.
What a lovely neo-romantic Moderato! Changing chro-

matic tonal harmonies and LH repeated chordal acc
reminiscent of Chopin's e minor Prelude.   Texture
often very close, with one hand over the other. Melodic coupling adds strength. (In 4.1, 2 pp.) Fngr,
MM.

5. 94 MEZÖ, IMRE.   Toccatina.
Accessible and brilliant Vivace. Technically useful for
measured trills in either hand, using fingers one and
two.   When LH trills, RH is rapid.   While centered
in aeolian mode on a, there are exotic chromatic
shifts up or down half tone. (In 4.8, 2 pp.) Fngr,
MM.

5. 95 MIYOSHI, AKIRA.   Suite in Such Time (1958).
Graceful, optimistic music, suitable for young in age
and spirit.   Resourceful textures include fairly wide
ranges, hands crossed and hands close to each other.
Tonal, with polyharmonies prominent.   Octave reach.
Comments in Japanese indicate that composer wrote
music to calm children following hint from program
by Japanese TV corporation.   So Merry Is Dabbling
(When One Isn't Fond of Bath-Taking) (I) moves Allegro and leggiero.   Much black key use, with pentatonic
hints and piquant harmonic shifts.   RH melody usually
legato, LH staccato.   Legato Andante Lions Live in
Far and Far (that is Far-Off) Lands (When One Asks
to be Taken Wild Beast Hunting) (IV) is lovely. High
broken-chord melody alternates with sustained gentle
sounds containing harmonic subtleties like double inflections.   Vivace, appassionamente For His Mama
(It May be Tea-Time) (V) is dashing and happy.
Fifths, broken octaves and the like bounce back and
forth between hands.   Translations of parenthetical
titles are (When One Doesn't Feel Like Sleeping) (II)
and (I Already Know That Story) (III). (In 5.4,
8 pp.) 5 movements. Some Ped. Ch. 5, some 4.

5. 96 MOMPOU, FEDERICO.   Chanson de Berceau.
Cradle Song has lovely purity of sound.   Prominent
thirds and sixths.   ABA in form, A is fuller in texture, and includes repetitions of two ninth chords with
lowered fifth; B is to be played with "tenderness."
Two measures before "Fin" are to be played only at
end.   Conservative. (In 5.2, 2 pp.) Some Fngr, MM.
Biog.

5.97 NIN-CULMELL, JOAQUIN. Tonados, Vol. 1 (1956).
Popular Melodies sound authentically Spanish. Have
traditional allure, and also more severe moods. Accs,
of fine pianistic resourcefulness, bring much appropriate character. Clear melodies. Added introduc-
tions and interludes. Have tenth reach. Included in
each title is province or city from which melody
comes. Translation and explanation of titles would be
helpful. Saratarra Naizela (1) has lovely simple melody in lilting 6/8. Bass uses only tonic and dominant
harmonies. Sweetness of doublings by sixths relieved
by sevenths, ninths, and the like. Jota (2) has irresistible melody, with usual triplet turns. Acc, with
pedal tones and bell-like effect, has expressive chromaticisms. In the brisk Dance (6) scale melody has
mixolydian tendencies. LH has quick lateral shifts for
broken chords. Bagpipe Dance (10) has flair and
bounce. Added-note dissonances give extra bite. Requires quick lateral shifts and ff playing. Melody of
Song of the Little Drum (11) has dotted note character,
LH acc adds staccato figure using shifting broken ninths
and sforzando syncopated chords. Gaiety of Children's
Nonsense Song (12) is brilliantly captured. Repeated
tones opening the melody used as accompanying motive;
also, the many fourths of melody are starting point for
ostinato added-note chord pattern. Translations (when
known) are Laborer's Song (3), Variations on the Ara-
da (5), Peasant Song (6), and Dance (7). (Ron, 1957,
17 pp.) 12 pieces. 15 min, 7 sec. MM, some Ped.
5 & 6.

5.98 NIN-CULMELL, JOAQUIN. Tonados, Vol. 2 (1957).
(See 5.97 for general remarks.) In Jota (13) the two-
phrase, six-note simple melody is accompanied by
cross rhythms between phrases and quick octave shifts.
Jota (18) is spontaneous in setting of transparent
simplicity. While the C melody is accompanied essentially by tonic and dominant harmonies, interest
comes from an aeolian scale fragment, a touch of
polyharmony and added-note chords. Much unnotated
alternations between 3/4 and 2/4. Mournful Autumn
Song (19) is a stepwise molto cantabile melody in f.
Dissonance is added to tonic-dominant ostinato by
added-note chords arranged as sevenths and by ninth
grace notes. Seguidilla (21) has traditional appeal.
One recurring measure's irregularity due to a different meter and harmony. RH has many staccato thirds.

Forearm and hand staccato. In the very slow Harvest
Song (22), the scale-wise melody with typical short
flourishes is accompanied by broken chords of effective
dissonance. Energetic drive of Bagpipe Dance (24)
never stops. Strong fingers needed for RH scale passages. LH acc vaults up and down keyboard with harmonic sevenths, ninths, and fifths. Uses tones only of
E, except for one short section. Translations (when
known) are Laborer's Song (14), Serenade (16), and
Muleteer's Song (23). (Ron, 1959, 22 pp.) 12 pieces,
14 min. MM, some Ped. 5, 6 & 7.

5.99 NORDOFF, PAUL. Hill Song.
Nostalgic folk mood. Seventh and ninth chords add
langorous fullness to pensive melody. In four voices,
with contrapuntal interest in secondary voices. To be
played "tenderly." (Pr. 1958, 2 pp.) Fngr, MM.
*Anal.

5.100 NØRGÅRD, PER. Sketches (1959).
Show special individuality. Keen phrase understanding
needed. Much is one-line music. Twelve-tone. Often no bar lines. Dynamics usually various shades of
p. Pedal directions not always clear. No stop between pieces. I, marked "freely flowing," moves in
up-and-down arabesques. In "capricious" II, the fanciful, fragmented acc is coupled with treble in rare pre-
cise unity. III, marked "moving," is in two sections;
B repeats the one-line music of A, but tones are now
grouped by chords. B moves "slowly, without strict-
ness," with "1 centimeter of page space lasting about
one and one-fourth second." Direction for IV is
"gracefully controlled." (WH, 1963, 2 pp.) 4 pieces.
Ped.

5.101 OKUMURA, H. Piano Melodies on Japanese Folk
        Songs.
Sympathetically and conservatively arranged. Predict-
ably, melodies tend to be in pentatonic mode. Super-
ficially, much repetition within melodies, but rarely
are whole sections repeated. Melody always in treble.
Composer's few additions to folk tunes are unobtrusive-
ly integrated. Some cross rhythms and ornaments.
Octaves and chords with added seconds used. Preface
in Japanese and English by composer, as well as biography and notes on background of each song. Cherry
Blossoms (1) sometimes in coupled writing. Decorated

version has rhythms of two against three. Beautiful
Adagio Folk Song from Village of Hokkaido (5) has
richly varied rhythm. Set in coupled writing or with
bass chords without thirds. Pentatonic mode on A, no
flats or sharps. Allegretto Song Celebrating Large
Catch of Fish (8) is simple and stolid. Acc rhythm
always long and two short. Acc has octaves with inner fifth, as well as fourths with added second. Boat
Song from Ondo (9) smoothly and traditionally arranged. Like a barcarole, with broken chord acc predominant. Uses only tones of aeolian mode on b, with
tones rarely outside pentatonic mode. Five-page Allegro Folk Song from Yagi District (12) is brilliant.
Tune, sometimes in octaves, is doubled or accompanied by various chordal ostinatos, contrasted by fan-
fare-like material in high register. Brilliance added
sometimes by polymodal, chordal acc. Chordal ostinatos not easy and require endurance. Translations
are Fisherman's Tune (2), Folk Song of the Island of
Sado (3), Mount Bandai in Aizu Province (4), Rice-
Planting Song (6), Lullaby of Ituski District (7), Folk
Song of Kiso District (10), and Folk Song of Tanchame
(11). (Ongaku, 1963, 33 pp.) 12 pieces. Fngr, MM,
some Ped. Biog. 5 & 6, some 4 & 7.

5.102 PALMER, ROBERT. Evening Music (1956).
Quietly masterful. Begins and ends with "flowing"
melody over contrapuntally activated harmonic acc. In
middle section 9/8 meter divided into groups of two,
three, two, and two. Modal. Dissonances handled securely. Many modulations at end. (Pr, 1958, 3 pp.)
Fngr, MM. *Anal.

5.103 PAPINEAU-COUTURE, JEAN. Valse I and II (1943,
1944).
Refined. First of the Two Waltzes marked modéré.
Prominent are accompanying fourth chords; excursions
in middle section into many flats, from a. Second
Waltz moves fast and flexibly. In C, with minor dominant often used; delightful modulations in middle section. RH often has three-note chords, LH usually
single notes which move lower for chord root. (In 8.1,
2 pp.) Some Fngr, MM & Ped.

5.104 PASCAL, CLAUDE. Animal Pageant.
Tuneful piece with customary march rhythms. Conservative harmonies relieved by a few out-of-key harmonies.

Needs strong RH fourth and fifth fingers for upper
tone of double notes. (In 3.6, 2 pp.) Fngr. Ch.

5.105 PENTLAND, BARBARA. Hands Across the C.
Sophisticated twelve-tone music. Foreword very helpful. "Three contrasting pieces ... range over all octaves of the piano so that neither hand is fenced-in by
middle C. Both hands are generally used as one,
passing the melody from one to the other. Since each
piece presents a certain technical problem, there is a
corresponding study...." Allegro giocoso Sparks flits
up and down the keyboard, repeating motives which include minor sevenths and ninths. In the veiled Mist
"the pedal joins the harmony tones, creating an atmosphere of mist and mystery." Single tones emphasized, and usually more than octave between preceding
and following tones. Seashore is in "a ternary form,
with the rolling tones of the first section inverted in
the last, and some cross-rhythms in the middle."
Many melodic fourths which may add up to tenth extension. (Wat, 1968, 10 pp.) 3 pieces. *Anal.

5.106 PENTLAND, BARBARA. Shadows-Ombres (1964).
Sombre expressionistic work, influenced by tone-row
technique; rises a few times to brief climaxes. Title
(Ombres is French for Shadows) illustrated by much
mirror writing. Has extreme registers. No repetition of ideas. Needs exact counting for note lengths
such as two successive dotted eighths or quarters in
4/4 meter. Minor ninth reach. Conveniently printed
so that all pages seen at one time. (Wat, 1968, 3
pp.) MM, Ped.

5.107 PERSICHETTI, VINCENT. Serenade No. 2, Op. 2.
Witty, sophisticated, and entertaining. Admirably economical. Phrasing fascinating in its variety. Tonal,
with all twelve tones most freely used, and unexpected
chords sometimes substituted for expected. Skillful
Tune has double notes used now with melody, now with
acc. Major sevenths in acc. Pluck is bright with
varied length slurs, effective syncopations and dynamic
changes. Title depicted by staccato common chords.
RH weaker fingers exercised. (EV, 1951, 6 pp.) 3
pieces. MM.

5.108 PHILLIPS, BURRILL. Five Various and Sundry.
Deft, often abstract works of some individuality. Pro-

grammatic titles. Very freely tonal, using all twelve
tones; some polyharmony. Three fast movements go
quickly indeed. Allegro ben ritmico Dialogue is between loud parallel polychord gestures and soft wide-
interval unaccompanied melody. Jaunty Allegro Trav-
eler often has RH melody of two alternating notes
against wandering LH series of first inversion minor
triads. Two-voice texture. In well-titled Jubilation,
RH scampers about in lively motion, often over four-
note ostinato. (EV, 1961, 5 pp.) MM, some Ped.
5 & 6.

5.109 PISK, PAUL A. Dance from the Rio Grande Valley.
Graceful Allegretto "based on an original Rio Grande
folk-melody." Often in three voices, with practice
for LH legato double notes. Middle section has added-
note chords. Fine practice for agility in RH weaker
fingers. (Mer, 1957--also 4.2, 3 pp.) Fngr. *Anal.

5.110 PLÉ, SIMONE. Fleurs d'Eau.
Romantic Water Flowers has lovely relaxed sounds.
Major tonality, often with raised fourth and lowered
seventh; many sharps and flats. No contemporary
problems. Useful for tone development and semi-ostinato wide-moving LH chords. (HL, 1958, 2 pp.)

5.111 PORTER, QUINCY. Day Dreams.
Lyrical appeal, with dissonances adding gentle coloring. Closely knit full sound, with up to five-tone
(eleventh) chords reached by small intervals and tied
tones. Careful tone balance developed. Exercises
RH fourth and fifth fingers. (Mer, 1958, 2 pp.)
Fngr. *Anal.

5.112 POULENC, FRANCIS. Le Petit Elephant, from
        L'Histoire de Babar.
The Little Elephant, from The Story of Babar, is
unassumingly charming. In A-flat, with ingratiating
(sometimes surprising) harmonies and full texture.
Rapid trill-like thirds, broken octaves and arpeggios.
Piece illustrates the quotation, "Babar tells her:
'Thank you, Madam'." Suitable also for older stu-
dents. Conservative. (In 3.6, 2 pp.) Some Fngr,
MM. Ch.

5.113 PREVIN, ANDRÉ. Impressions for Piano.
Clever and attractive fare for those who prefer famil-

iar sounds. Improvising facile pianist's fingers often
seem to direct. Unusual treatment of usual harmonies
--quick chord shifts, remote modulations, or polyharmonies, in Prokofieff manner. Octave reaches and
similar extensions. Some titles suitable only for children. Gay Good Morning is in plainest C, but with innovations like opening dominant seventh chord colored
by b-flat, c, and f-sharp. In high register. Polar
Bear Dance begins with dissonance, but soon resolves
to dominant of C. Bounces from register to register.
Thoughtful Trees at Twilight has seventh and ninth
chords. High-spirited Round-Up has syncopated open
fifth acc and white-key melody with black-key acc.
The Out-of-Tune Band is depicted by logical chromatic
or whole tone progress in acc, but melody usually
doesn't cooperate! (P 9, 14, 18, & 20.) (Leeds-NY,
1964, 22 pp.) 20 pieces. Some Fngr, MM. 5, some
4 & 6.

5.114 QUINET, MARCEL. Enfantines (1959).
Have individuality and growing appeal. Certainly not
exclusively Children's Pieces. Mild exoticism from
predominance of small melodic intervals colored by
wandering chromaticism. Patterns reiterated before
moving on; whole is economical. Tonal, with free use
of all twelve tones. Many harmonic seconds. Most
often in two-voice texture, one voice leading. Ryth-
mically traditional. Prelude begins and ends with fanfare; main section has RH fairly fast scalar melody
and varied acc, sometimes suggesting polyharmony.
Spontaneous Gavotte has delightful harmonic play and
much staccato. Near-ostinato LH acc alternates between single tone and third or second. Hands alternate in busy Toccata, with predominant shifting by LH.
Idiomatic to the piano and a joy to play. (CBDM,
1959, 14 pp.) 6 pieces. 7 min, 10 sec. MM. 5,
some 4.

5.115 REIZENSTEIN, FRANZ. Study in Irregular Rhythms.
Facile neo-classic Allegretto grazioso of transparently
clear aims. Meters range from 3/8 through 9/8, often changing each measure, not difficult to master.
Lively variety between staccato and legato articulation.
Harmonies blithely roam through flats and sharps while
firmly anchored in D. (Oxf, 1962, 3 pp.) Fngr.

5.116 RIVIER, JEAN.   The Little Gondolier.
Has gentle melancholy.   Tonal harmonies of e-flat are
mildly "wrong," as if melody or acc were misplaced
by a tone.   RH has parallel legato thirds and second
inversion triads.   LH uses extended broken triads.
(In 5.1, 2 pp.)   Fngr, MM.

5.117 ROREM, NED.   A Quiet Afternoon (1948).
Warmly lyrical collection with some originality.   Appealing simplicity and gentleness.   Pedal very important, especially to aid legato double notes.   Ninth
reaches.   Key signatures through five sharps and three
flats.   Titles may suggest works are for children, but
really more suitable for adolescents.   Allegro A New
Game has melody of graceful rise and fall.   Pure
mixolydian mode on G for beginning and ending gives
way to many sharps in middle section.   Lonesome
Waltz, marked "poignant," has moderately wide-range
and wide-interval treble RH melody.   In D lydian mode.
The Tiny Tin Dancers provides experience among black
keys.   Prominent LH broken chord pattern ends on
major seventh.   Evening Rainbow, marked "warm and
calm," shows pandiatonic influences with prominent
fourths and fifths.   Numerous legato double notes in
each hand.   (Peer, 1951, 11 pp.)   9 pieces.   5, some
4 & 6.

5.118 RUEFF, JEANINE.   Vacances, Vol. 2.
Holidays shows French suavity, brightness, and taste.
Varied kinds of writing now considered conservative:
harmony of seventh, ninth, and added-note chords, as
well as many modulations which give practice in keys
through E, c-sharp, g-sharp and E flat.   Some meter
changes.   Idiomatic piano writing.   Few reaches beyond a seventh.   Moderately fast tempos predominate.
Usually only titles indicate music is for children.   The
Allegretto giocoso Picnic in the Woods (14) has variety
of articulations.   Shifts between 6/8 and 5/8 meters,
as well as a few appearances of 3/4 in the 6/8 measures.   LH acc has staccato parallel chords and arpeggios.   The Presto Let Us Dance the Round (15) is
direct and simple, like a folk dance.   Moves from G
through C, G-flat, C-flat, E-flat, D-flat, and back to
G.   Many meter shifts from 2/8 through 5/8.   Allegro Chase (16) is skillful two-voice canon.   Rhythmic
distance between voices changes from two beats to one
to one-half.   Only a few accidentals, unusual for col-

lection. Also unusual, Polka (19) has wide-interval
treble melody, requiring ninth legato reach. Staccato
polka acc moves widely between changing low single
tones and upper three-tone chords. Translations are
Kapy, the Little Squirrel (11), A Beautiful Story (12),
The House Covered with Ivy (13), The Pond with the
Red Fish (17), The Hive (18), and In the Evening
Everyone Sleeps (20). (Led, 1968, 18 pp.) 10 pieces.
MM. Ch. 5 & 6.

5.119 SAEVERUD, HARALD. Sonatina, Op. 30, No. 5.
Inventive music, "quasi una fantasia," communicates
well. Movements connected without pause. Allegretto
is exquisitely tender with very fanciful ending. Much
use of opening motive. Moderato has double note LH
acc; in contrast, rest of Sonatina usually only two
voices. Bright spirited Allegro assai is soft, "but
marked," and non legato. Has sudden outbursts.
Closing Allegretto has delicate single note alternation
between hands, with material from first and second
movements. (In 6.5, 5 pp.) 4 movements. MM.
Biog.

5.120 SANTA CRUZ, DOMINGO. Childhood Images, Series
2, Op. 13b.
Expressive work, as suitable for older performers as
for children. Dissonant chromatic tonal harmony with
many double inflections. Titles also in Spanish. Na
Pancha's Song is leisurely. Three inflections of third
of chord in quick succession indicate chromatic harmony. Texture in three and four voices, main voice
in RH; LH uses extended broken chords. Keen musical intelligence and wit in The Mischievous Boy. Melody accompanied by repeated two and three-tone intervals (changing chromatically) alternates between hands.
(Peer, 1960, 8 pp.) 4 pieces. MM.

5.121 SATIE, ERIK. Deux Rêveries Nocturnes (1910-11).
(See 4.130.) Two Nocturnal Dreams, exquisitely
French, have moderate speed and supple rubato. I is
unbarred, improvisatory. Voice leading determines
flexible harmonies. Prevailing texture is LH single
line and RH three-note broken chord. It shifts first
to parallel motion and then merges into "a little
faster" single line arabesque. First direction is
"gently dream." II is pure music. Has delightful
mixture of repeated fragments in many guises and

newly composed progressions.   Quite chromatic.
Translations on p 3 are "very gentle," "moving
ahead," and "a tempo."   Revised by R. Caby.   (Sal,
1968, 4 pp.)   3 min, 50 sec.   MM.

5.122 SATIE, ERIK.   Musiques Intimes et Secrètes.
(See 4.130.)   Fine works in Intimate and Secret Music.   Counterpoint and some texture variety.   Revised
by R. Caby who, in a foreword in French, suggests
joining these with three from Six Pieces (see 5.125).
Nostalgia always has two measures in two voices and
two measures in full chordal setting.   Phrases end in
e, G, and A.   Cold Reverie (p 3), marked "a little
slow," has chromatic harmony.   Ends inconclusively.
Unfortunate Example (p 4) is a splendid study for legato playing in three-part counterpoint.   Middle voice
always whole notes.   In pure b.   Footnote indicates
that Caby wrote the last five measures.   (Sal, 1968,
3 pp.)   3 pieces.   5, some 4.

5.123 SATIE, ERIK.   Quatrieme Gnossienne (1891).
(See 4.130.)   Fourth Gnossienne is a soft, slow mono-
chrome, marked "without hurry."   Title may allude to
palace of Knossos in Crete.   Treble has parlando
(speaking) phrases of short durations, separated by
rests.   Mostly stepwise melodies sometimes end with
surprise, like a tritone.   RH always has arpeggios.
Modal progressions of minor chords by seconds, except in two striking exceptions.   (Sal, 1968, 2 pp.)
3 min, 33 sec.   MM.

5.124 SATIE, ERIK.   Sixieme Gnossienne (1897).
(See 4.130 and 5.123.)   Sixth Gnossienne is a lyrical
number of moderate speed to be played "with convic-
tion and with a rigorous sadness."   Five ideas, from
three to eight beats long, are freely transposed and
fascinatingly reordered as work progresses.   LH, always moving in eighth notes, usually has a broken
chord extending a tenth.   Only sixteenths, eighths, and
quarters.   Bar lines omitted.   (Sal, 1968, 2 pp.)   1
min, 20 sec.   MM.

5.125 SATIE, ERIK.   Six Pieces (1906-13).
(See 4.130.)   Texture variety from simple three-part
counterpoint to octave reinforced homophonic texture
with added secondary contrapuntal activity.   Pure tonality, but also considerable chromaticism.   Thematic

development uncommon to Satie. R. Caby, who revised three of the works, writes in a preface in
French: "This disconsolate music, from a solitary
man tempered by an overabundance of serene kindness,
will perhaps remind one of certain pages of J.S. Bach
as well as some excerpts from Beethoven's adagios in
the last quartets." Effrontery (II) fascinates by rear-
ranging transpositions and successions of three basic
ideas; there is also a sequence. Lovely Poetry (III)
is resourceful in its variety: (a) chordal addition to
coupled writing, (b) grace notes, (c) sudden harmonic
shifts, and (d) break into short ad libitum passage.
Direction translations are "fairly blue," "as in a
cloister," "whiter," and "flowing." Canine Prelude
(IV) has skillful flexibility of texture. Both tonal and
modal harmony. No key signature. Translations are
Pleasant Unhappiness (I), Profundity (V), and Dreamer
(VI). (Sal, 1968, 8 pp.) Some Fngr & MM. 5,
some 4 & 6.

5.126 SAUGUET, HENRI. La Chanson du Soir.
Evening Song is an expert pastel, colors blurred together by pedal ("change each measure"). RH leads
in two-voice texture. Melody often suspended on added second, while acc touches added sixth. Conservative. (In 8.2, 2 pp.) Fngr, MM, Ped.

5.127 SAYGUN, A. ADNAN. From Anatolia.
Exotic, well-constructed works. (Anatolia is western
Asia Minor.) Skillful, traditional pianistic writing.
Meseli is in 9/8--two, two, two, and three. Small
interval treble melody in dorianlike mode with lowered
fifth; thus, includes augmented second. Repetitive acc
pattern centered on pedal tone alternating with small
cluster chords. Halay is brilliant concert work with
pianistic flair. In six sections, work begins with two-
voice polymodal texture and builds to full-texture rapid octave sections and presto scalar conclusion. Only
last two sections are thematically related. (P 5.)
(Peer, 1957, 13 pp.) 3 pieces. MM, some Ped. 5
& 8.

5.128 SCHÄFER, KARL. Drei Burlesken (1952).
Three Burlesques are effective novelty works with solid content. I has jazzy syncopations. Parallel sevenths of near-ostinato acc against melody using fourths
and fifths suggest tonal music. II is twelve-tone La-

mentoso with minor seconds, minor sevenths, and major ninths. Textures of angular melody with double
note acc or canon at major ninth. III is an Allegro
giocoso scintillating with glassy dissonances. Twelve-
tone set order often changed. Equal hand emphasis,
needing finger agility on simultaneous trills and rapid
passage work with extensions. (Noet, 1960, 6 pp.)
4 min, 15 sec. MM. 5, 6 & 7.

5.129 SCHÄFER, KARL. Miniaturen (1959).
Imaginative and varied Miniatures. Combines German
mastery of form and counterpoint with French charm
and taste. Fast and staccato numbers of scherzo nature are best. Tonal, with all twelve tones freely
used. Often in three-part form. More music than
usual on printed page. III is perpetual motion Allegro
scherzando. Polyrhythms and changes of measure
lengths indicate constant rhythmic interest. Hands often alternate. Finger staccato used. V, marked
"pesante," is a near expressionistic passacaglia with
theme using eleven different tones. As climax builds,
theme is embedded in coupled two-part writing, followed by theme in octaves accompanied by RH parallel
sevenths. VIII is a bittersweet Grazioso in rubato
waltz step. Much harmonic piquancy with treble clashing over repeated LH harmonies; ends with V/I chord.
IX is sober, intense, and dissonant Andante. Declamatory repeated chords (up to thirteenths) move in parallel or contrary motion. Includes rapid runs and trills.
X is playful Allegretto. Six-note motive developed over
ostinatolike bass, or treated imitatively, or rhythmically diminished in cadenzalike two-part Piu mosso section. (P 2 & 5.) (Noet, 1960, 16 pp.) 11 pieces.
14 min. MM. 5 & 6, some 4.

5.130 SCHMIDT, Y. RUDNER. Miniatures Lobateanas
        (1964-67).
Attractive Miniatures After Lobato are deft evocations
of Brazilian popular music, inspired by tales of writer,
Lobato. Pieces usually in rhythm or mood of native
dance or song. Habanera rhythm frequent. Splendid
analysis in Portuguese summarizes features of folk elements. Skillful textures are moderately full, with careful use of double notes and LH extensions. Some titles
might restrict music to children. The few modernisms
no deterrent to this appealing music. Story of Aunt
Nastácia (2) a Modinha, "popular song usually of amor-

ous inspiration." In first section LH has counter melody with numerous extensions; RH has legato sixths in second section. Ending is "frisky." Dream of Emilia (3) a graceful waltz. Each hand has moderately fast single note passages in flexible patterns. Augmented seconds. Final minor chord has added second and tritone. Triumph of Dona Benta (4), a Baião, "original dance from northeast Brazil," is pleasant salon-type work. RH offbeat, small cluster accompanying chords. Each hand hops about some. In Country of the Chestnut-Winged Yellow Wood Pecker (9), a Jongo dance played "without haste." RH "weeping" melody uses parallel thirds for "singer and accompaniment" and "chorus of dancers;" LH semi-ostinato patterns use double notes with one part held while other moves. Translations are The Classroom of Viscount Sabugosa (1), marked "without hurry;" The Marquis of Rabicó (5), "fastidious" and "imposing;" Pranks of Little Peter (6), "not too fast;" Jeca-Tatu (fictitious name for typical hillbilly) (7), "weeping," "like a kind of guitar," "a little joyful," and "hopeful;" and Pranks of Little Snub Nose (8). (IVi, 1967, 19 pp.) 9 pieces. Fngr. *Anal. 5, some 4.

5.131 SCHMIT, CAMILLE. Rigaudon.
Mischievous. Brightly neo-classic. Full of irregularities: melodies are repeated with different order or added counter melody, unexpected accents, harmonic shifts. Forearm staccatos. (In 5.1, 2 pp.) Fngr, MM.

5.132 SCHOLLUM, ROBERT. Acht kleine Klavierstücke, Op. 54b (1956).
Eight Small Pieces reveal lively musical intelligence. Serial procedures used some, with set fragments repeated. Traditional in rhythmic patterns, repeated motives, medium ranges, and common styles (such as waltz, theme and variations, and chorale). Clear musical gestures (helped by editing) aid in comprehension of form. Much linear counterpoint. Directions in German. In III, after "grazioso" waltz rhythm is established, moderate changes of meter occur. Fluent treble melody often returns to same tone to aid rhythmic feel. "Very fast and light" V is clear in musical progress: passage repetition or exceptional coupled writing indicate section ending; ostinato accompanies long crescendo with treble ascent; less ac-

tivity at end, etc. Non-tonal, although G is suggested
at end. VII a theme and three variations (with return
to theme at end) "in a quiet step." Theme has two
phrases, with frequent two-note slurs. Variations almost disguise theme. Main material in VIII, "broadly
flowing (like a chorale)," stated in first two phrases
in chordal texture. Material restated throughout, with
style and tempo changes. Has common chords. (Dob,
1957, 11 pp.) MM. 5 & 6.

5.133 SCHUMAN, WILLIAM. Three Piano Moods: I Lyrical (1958).
"Flowing legato melody played expressively and freely."
Melody fascinatingly varied; has wide leaps and no
repetitions. Traditional ostinato bass descending a
fourth. (Mer, 1959, 2 pp.) Fngr, MM. *Anal.

5.134 SESSIONS, ROGER. Little Piece (1939).
Enticing Allegro has straightforward treble tune in C.
Acc, freely introducing accidentals, alternates between
slower two-note intervals and agile scale passages.
(In 4.1, 1 p.) Biog.

5.135 SLAVICKÝ, KLEMENT. Piano and Youth.
Fluent musical imagination. Unobtrusive new uses of
familiar techniques is in splendid taste and should
bother no one. Works increase in difficulty. Both
modal and tonal. Titles also in German and Czech.
Preludium long-lined Allegro with fine forward motion.
Unified, partly by many melodic thirds. In 8/8 meter,
usually three, two, and three. RH leads in two-voice
texture. Bouncing, Allegretto giocoso Czech Song has
varied articulations. Uses forearm strokes on accents
and staccatos. In D. The Foresaken Bird poignantly
portrayed by realistic chirps outlining tritone and by
lyrical writing using legato parallel sixths and broken
chords (often on black keys). "Animato, con ele-
ganzia" aptly characterizes neo-romantic A Melanchol-
ic Waltz. Gives splendid practice in mildly extended
and adventurous intervals, particularly on black keys.
In f-sharp. Marked "calmo," A Ballad (also in 4.7)
is moderately sophisticated salon-type piece. Warm
chromatic tonal harmony--one measure may have many
sharps and next many flats. LH has extended broken
chords. Middle Appassionato portion more difficult
with two and three moving parts. (Pan, 1966, 13 pp.)
10 pieces. Fngr, MM, Ped. 5, some 4 & 6.

5.136 SMITH, HALE. Evocation.
Moderately slow twelve-tone work of strong, clear character. Varied dynamics. Flexible rhythms like rapid
quintuplets for half or whole beats. Doublings give
full sonority. Ninth reach. (Pet 6875, 1965--also in
5.3, 3 pp.) MM, some Ped.

5.137 SMITH, LELAND. Four Etudes (1952).
Twelve-tone works of character and variety. No quick
appeal; no facile pianism. Textures divided between
polyphony and homophony. Ranges, dynamics, and tempos are moderate. Graceful III, marked "dance-like,"
often has dotted thirds. Moves stringendo to ff climax.
IV, marked "decisive," is faster than other Etudes.
Flexible texture--sometimes two voices, sometimes
four-tone chords. Two motives recur. (Mer, 1966,
4 pp.) MM. 5 & 6.

5.138 SOMMERFELDT, ØISTEIN. Miniature-Suite.
Works have youthful aspect: optimistic (neo-classic) or
sentimental (neo-romantic). Modernisms are slight,
with harmonic charm of chromaticisms and modulations
most noticeable. Titles also in Norwegian and German.
Melody of Waltz has graceful roll. Traditional acc.
Middle section settles in b-flat and ends in e; otherwise
pleasant chromatic wandering. Hard-Head is energetic
and bright sounding. Much staccato upbeat skipping to
held downbeat, tones then spreading wider by chromatic
motion. ABA form. (Norsk, 1959, 10 pp.) 5 pieces.

5.139 SOUTHAM, ANN. Quodlibet.
A Quodlibet combines well-known melodies "in an ad-
visedly incongruous manner." This is partially illustrated by irregular treble rhythm against steady bass,
and by poly-chords between hands. Nimble RH phrases,
with much broken chord outline, often end just before
a main beat. Near-ostinato acc uses some changing
second inversion chords each beat, often a third apart.
(BMI, 1967, 2 pp.) MM, Ped.

5.140 SOUTHAM, ANN. Sea Flea.
Fluent and gay Vivacissimo. In two-part texture. Each
hand often momentarily in five finger position, only to
jump about over moderately wide range. Flickerings
of quick modulations and polytonality. (BMI, 1963, 2
pp.) Fngr.

5.141 SOUTHAM, ANN. Three in Blue.
Remarkably spontaneous and attractive jazz preludes in
fast tempos. Three pieces to be played "attacca."
Allegretto I has blues characteristics of variable third
and seventh degrees, which also appear in cross relationship. Fine unity. Andantino II swings nonchalant-
ly in 9/8. Has added-note chords, as well as LH
wailing fourths and fifths. III an Allegro ma non troppo. High-spirited and sophisticated. Often a walking
staccato bass. Touch and dynamic variety. (BMI,
1966, 9 pp.) MM. 5, some 6.

5.142 STARER, ROBERT. Three Israeli Sketches.
Accessible, and richly imaginative. Tonal, freely using all twelve tones. Of neo-classic leaning, thin in
texture. Rhythms alive with varied note lengths and
slurring. Beautiful Pastorale sounds Oriental in its
improvisatory melody. Melody has from two to eight
tones each beat. In ABA form with B of fuller texture
and last A harmonized differently. Dance, neatly vigorous and spontaneous, is Allegro giocoso. Treble
melody only. Acc of parallel fifths or secondary
voice. Meter predominantly 2/4, varied by 5/8 and
2/8. Prominent rests. (MCA, 1957, 8 pp.) Some
Fngr, MM.

5.143 STROHBACH, SIEGFRIED. Die Spielzeugkiste (1952).
Play Box pieces are delightfully naive. Familiar materials used with moderate differences. German in
character. Textures are homophonic; same rhythm for
melody and acc in two works. No legato reach beyond
seventh; larger staccato leaps. Allegro, leggiero
Tumbler Doll (1) is extrovert. Legato double notes in
each hand, with frequent parallel motion. Meters often change from 3/8 through 6/8. Andante sostenuto
Rolling Sailing Ship (3) is pentatonic, using black keys.
Against LH rolling acc, RH melody is flutelike and
rhythmically improvisatory (notated in 6/4) with many
fourths and fifths. The Block Tower (4) is square-cut
in melody with whole, half, and quarter notes only.
Acc common chords are in arbitrary successions.
Translations are Dancing Teddy Bear (2), The Rocking
Horse (5), and The Jumping Jack (6). (Br&H 6209,
1955, 10 pp.) 6 pieces. MM. Ch. 5, some 6.

5.144 SYDEMAN, WILLIAM. Prelude.
"Slow and heavy" abstract study in chords. Atonal,

with numerous major seconds and major sevenths; cross relations. When repeated, first seven measures are varied by general augmentation or other rhythmic change. (In 4.1, 1 p.) Ped. Biog.

5.145 SZOKOLAY, SANDOR. Szonatine.
Optimistic and filled with imaginative ideas. Mildly exploratory work in C. Piano writing has much variety. Opening Allegro con brio, appropriately subtitled "Capriccio," has coupled writing, texture in which LH support is rhythmically irregular, and marcato chord strokes. Two-voiced "Ostinato andante" movement moves attacca to Allegro giocoso finale. Among types of writing are two voices with independent rhythmic interest in LH acc, alternating hands with LH stationary, and some range shifting. In treble range. Last movement conservative. (In 4.10, 5 pp.) 3 movements. Fngr. 5, some 4.

5.146 TEPKOV, DIMITER. Grandfather's Glove.
Lively and spontaneous musical impulse propels this Allegro spirituoso. Melody, which may be a folk tune, changes upon repetition from mixolydian to aeolian mode. Many two-note slurs, and much dynamic interest. Harmonies moderately chromatic. Metronome mark must be for half note. Prefaced by quote: "Grandfather went to Slatitz and lost his glove." (In 4.3, 2 pp.) MM. *Biog.

5.147 THOMSON, VIRGIL. Portraits, Album 4 (1935-1942).
Refreshingly bright and witty. Lovely naive music provides experience with polytonality, polyharmony, and dissonant counterpoint. At times unusually consonant. Disparate elements often combined in one work. Very complete fingering. For each Portrait "the subject sits for his likeness as he would for a painter; and the music is composed in front of him, usually at one sitting." Several works are witty, two (and portions of two others) are very consonant and immediately pleasing. Direction "senza pedale" given several times. Poltergeist (translated Noisy Fellow): A Portrait of Hans Arp portrays title with humorous and audacious details, such as unexpected leaps, swift dissonant two-voice writing in high register, increases in dynamics, speed, and polyharmony. Insistences: A Portrait of Louise Crane has canons in two voices in two different places, naturally depicting title; added in-

sistence from lightly repeated, doubly inflected chords
and polychords. Only seven tones of A-flat used in
the most joyous Molto ritmico Wedding Music: A Portrait of Jean Watts. Fresh, even if traditional.
Moves from melody and broken chord texture to three
and four voices, then to stately three-voice chords,
ending in fuller texture. (Merc--assigned to GS, 1953,
22 pp.) 8 pieces. Fngr, MM. 5, 6 & 7.

5.148 TOCH, ERNST. Diversions, Op. 78a.
Often very beautiful. Will appeal to serious, mature
musicians. Tonal, using all twelve tones freely; useful for pianistic flexibility among black keys. Edition
unusually helpful with fingering. Usually in two-voice
texture (linear counterpoint), although not usually imitative. III, even though marked "tranquillo," builds
impressively to climaxes through compelling lines,
treble leading. Harmony very secondary. IV, a leggiero, poco mosso, has splendid verve. Many two-
note slurs. Accessible, with clear harmony and pleasing chromaticism. (Leeds-NY, 1958, 9 pp.) 5 pieces.
Fngr, MM. 5 & 6.

5.149 TOCH, ERNST. Sonatinetta, Op. 78b.
Consistent neo-classic work of extrovert appeal. Lean
texture, most often in two voices. Tonal, freely using
all twelve tones; fluent piano writing wanders easily
among black and white keys. First movement, marked
"Allegro and gay," is sparked by percussive added-note
chords and varied articulations. Second movement
lovely and natural Andante semplice. In unusually consonant two-part texture. Closing Allegro is witty. Sonata form without development and without recapitulation
of second theme, as in first movement. (Leeds-NY,
1958, 5 pp.) 3 movements. Fngr, MM. 5, some 4.

5.150 TROJAN, VÁCLAV. The Bells of Prague.
Study in chordal sonorities. Colorful sounds created
with different harmonies realistically blended by pedal.
(Pedal lengths may be confusing.) Fine variety of ma-
terial. Full texture. (In 4.7, 2 pp.) Some Ped.
*Biog.

5.151 TSUKATANI, Y. Sakura Sakura, Edo Komoriuta,
    Chūgokuchihō No Komoriuta, Hirosaki Shishimai-
    Odori, Yagi Bushi and Aizu Bandaisan.
Direct appeal, whether quiet or brilliant. As usual,

harmonic seconds, fourths and fifths (not thirds) prominent. Melodies in a two-half step pentatonic scale,
with first three on same pitch. Lovely Cherry Blossom, Cherry Blossom (p 6) is "like a nocturne." Between simple statements of melody whole step apart
there are flourishes of exotically colored broken treble
chords. Lullaby from Edo (p 8) and Lullaby from
District of Chogoku (p 9) are most sensitive. In both,
second setting of melody imaginatively varied. First
marked Adagio, but may be "andante or lento;" second
directed to be "rubato." Lion Dance from Hirosako
(p 24) and Melody from Yagi (p 26) are brilliant, extrovert works propelled by varied percussive thrusts.
In first, LH forearm stabs give drum beats, to which
is added RH in second number. Latter is indeed
"healthy," "humorous," and "capricious." RH has
rapid repeated tones. Allegro moderato Mount Aizu
Bandai Dance (p 28) aims to help people to "work
well;" it is "clean and simple." Melody has single
tones, or is coupled. Each hand alternates in simple
rhythmic acc using hand staccatos. (In 6.3, 2 pp, 1
p, 1 p, 2 pp, 2 pp, & 3 pp.) Anal. 5, 4, 5, 7, 7,
& 5.

5.152 VERRAL, JOHN. Sketches and Miniatures (1954).
Quiet, witty works of refinement and polished craftsmanship. Lively rhythms. Graceful melodies. Contrapuntal imitation important in half the numbers.
Freely tonal. Allegretto Prelude I admirably builds
in swirls to small climaxes. Tones in 5/8 are flexibly grouped by two and three, the reverse, etc.
Vivace Fughetta I is not too serious about itself because subject is frequently omitted. Merriment starts
immediately with double inflections of both first and
third of scale. Activity continues with angular episodes and chromatic thicknesses successfully resolved.
Pianistic playfulness in every measure of the Allegretto. Constant bouncing back and forth between hands.
Broken chords in RH. Measure lengths often vary between five and seven eighths. Arietta is lyrical and
homophonic. Several minor seventh chords indicate
harmony more traditional than usual, but final triad is
doubly inflected. Percussive and mildly dissonant
Bizarria spontaneously rolls along Allegro molto. Fine
unity. (VMP, 1955, 14 pp.) 10 pieces. MM, some
Ped. 5, some 6.

5.153 WAGNER-RÉGENY, RUDOLF.   Zwei Klavierskizzen.
Two Piano Sketches use obvious twelve-tone technique.
Same set used for both works: first Sketch, in original order, second Sketch in retrograde order, returning to original order at end.   Emphasis given to first
or last tone of set for tonal impression.   Hands treated equally.   Ninth reach necessary.   Expressive melody in I.   Texture has much variety.   Three different
double notes often used for acc.   Fine climaxes.   II
has clear phrases, each phrase stating set once.
Wide range melody alternates with fanfare of ninths.
Invertible counterpoint.   (In 8.3, 3 pp.) Biog.

5.154 WEBER, BEN.   New Adventure.
An Andante espressivo with growing appeal.   Needs
emotional intensity and freedom.   Distantly tonal.
Uses firmer weight touch on weaker fingers and soft
acc on stronger fingers.   For the most dedicated.
(Mer, 1957, 2 pp.) Fngr, Ped. *Anal.

5.155 WEISGALL, HUGO.   Sine Nomine (1966).
Cantabile Without Name has elusive appeal--performer
must seek it.   Gentle expression requires rubato.
Usually RH has double notes, most often major sevenths or seconds.   LH acc has varied broken intervals.   Individual lines more diatonic than chromatic,
but little evidence of tonality.   Originally written for
TV documentary. (Pr, 1968, 2 pp.) MM.

5.156 WILLIAMSON, MALCOLM.   Travel Diaries, Paris,
      Vol. 4.
(See 4.165.) Only more modern compositions chosen
for review in this more conservative volume.   Cus-
toms has non-stop "fast as possible" RH broken chord
acc: excellent for rotary motion with endurance. Bass
jabs humorously incongruous.   (Bass, when played
backwards in last piece, proves to be Au Clair de la
Lune forwards!)   Freedom of arm motion encouraged
in staccato forte measures of Poco presto Gendarme.
RH uses broken chord extending an octave.   Clusters
give realistic sounds of horns.   Chantlike melody,
aeolian mode (on c-sharp), and open fifths arouse medieval feeling of Notre Dame Cathedral.   5/2 meter.
In "slow, dreamy" Boat Ride Down the Seine, RH has
slight extensions in three-tone legato chords.   Exercise for RH weaker fingers.   Much whole tone or rapid RH chromatic writing in Allegro The Eiffel Tower.

(Chap-L 45909, 1962, 14 pp.) 10 pieces. Fngr,
MM, Ped. *Anal. 5, some 4.

5.157 WILSON, THOMAS. <u>Reverie</u>.
Of mild exotic character. Fine unity. Uses ground
bass made up of two broken chords half step apart,
based on "foreign" tonic pedal. Requires equal soft
touch from most of LH fingers. Middle faster section,
with agility in both hands, is polyharmonic. (Ric-L,
1961, 3 pp.) 2 min, 35 sec. Fngr, Ped.

5.158 WIRÉN, DAG. <u>Miniatyr</u> (1962).
<u>Miniature</u>, marked "calmo," has lingering plaintive
mood. Simple stately measures have many triplets.
No thumb under. Ground bass. Some invertible
counterpoint. (In 5.5, 1 p.) MM.

5.159 YAMADA, KAZUO. <u>Sonatina</u> (1943).
Delightful brightness with enough harmonic modernities
to arouse attention. Tuneful melodies abound, as do
syncopations. Splendid craftsmanship. Neo-classic.
Important comments, in Japanese, tell of composer's
hope that work will be performed in simple and blithe
spirit. Moderato in clear sonata form. Tonic harmony, with and without raised root, hints at slight
harmonic adventures. Andante is like folk song; in E-
flat, contrasting with earlier and later G. In middle
section Molto cantabile melody has short-long rhythms,
while LH acc (hands crossed) repeats Oriental-sounding
tones. Traditional rondo's high spirits in Allegro final
movement. Main theme marked by syncopated raised
fourth scale tone. Translation of directions on p 49
are "merrily" and "rather slowly," p 51 "slowly" and
"deeply," p 53 "deeply expressive," p 54 "dreamily,"
p 56 "rather slowly and naively" and "a little faster,"
and p 57 "lightly." (In 5.4, 9 pp.) 3 movements.
Fngr, MM, Ped.

5.160 ZBINDEN, JULIEN-FRANÇOIS. <u>Quatre Solitudes,</u>
        Op. 17 (1951).
<u>Four Solitudes</u> collection is effective piano writing,
with clear-cut profile, even originality. III, a lovely
Lento "with an unusual serenity," is nicely varied:
two-part linear counterpoint, as well as incidental
polyphony; also sonorous chords, both the usual and
polychords. "With an ambiguous indifference" is indication for IV, an Allegrissimo. Clever neo-classic

play with tonalities.   Rapid scales and arpeggios in RH
effective and great fun to play.   II is directed to be
played "with a desperate energy."   (P 2.)   (Zer, 1955,
15 pp.)   11 min, 30 sec.   MM.   5, some 7 & 8.

DATA FROM VOLUME II   Pertinent to Volume I

6.3   Japanese Folk Air(s) on the Piano.
Sympathetic arrangements of folk melodies by Itō,
Koyama, Makino, and Tsukatani.   All pieces reviewed.
(See 5.151, 6.76, 6.89 and 6.101.)   Fine balance between literal statements of melody and pianistic additions in spirit of melody.   Melodies, in a pentatonic
scale with usually two half steps, are almost always
in treble.   Cluster elements in accs, with substitu-
tions for third of chord.   Commentaries by composers
in Japanese offer sociological background and some analysis.   (Zen, 1960, 47 pp.)   13 pieces.   Some MM.
*Anal.   6, some 4, 5, 7 & 8.

6.5   Nordisk Klavermusik, Ny.
New Northern Piano Music contains sonatinas by three
Danish, two Finnish, one Norwegian, and six Swedish
composers.   Eight works reviewed.   (See 4.127,
5.119, 6.14, 6.94, 6.97, 7.96, 8.12, and 8.43.)
Contains music by Bentzon, Bergman, de Frumerie,
Høffding, von Koch, Larsson, Lidholm, Palmgren,
Riisager, Rosenberg, Saeverud, and Wirén.   Included
are pictures of the composers, a biography in the composer's native language, and comments by the composer on the music.   (Geh, 1951, 133 pp.)   13 sonatinas,
12 composers.   Some MM & Ped.   Biog.   6 & 8, some
4, 5 & 7.

6.6   Pepparrot, ed by Birgitta Nordenfelt.
Fine variety in Horseradish (title has only personal
significance), subtitled New Scandinavian Piano Music.
Nine works reviewed.   (See 4.122, 5.82, 6.17, 6.63,
6.65, 6.96, 6.130 and 6.131.)   Most works are tonal and
fairly conservative.   Contains music by Blomdahl,
Bäck, Holmboe, Høffding, Lidholm, Riisager, and
Saeverud.   Foreword, biographies, and titles in Swedish, English, and German.   (Nord, 1951, 37 pp.)   16

pieces, 7 composers. Usually Fngr & MM, some
Ped. Biog. 6, some 4 & 5.

8.1   Canadian Composers, Fourteen Piano Pieces By.
      Fast and witty numbers are particularly appealing.
      Ten pieces are thought worthy of review, a high per-
      centage. (See 3.23, 3.29, 4.84, 5.15, 5.103, 6.111,
      7.21, 8.15, 8.27 and 8.89.) Seven pieces are
      selections from larger works. More music than aver-
      age is on each page. Chosen for Canadian League of
      Composers by pianists and teachers Roubakine, Kilburn,
      and Moss. Foreword, biographies, and factual mater-
      ial on music is included in English and French. Con-
      tains music by Beckwith, Betts, Blackburn, Brott,
      Coulthard, Dolin, Fleming, Freedman, Kasemets,
      Morawetz, Morel, Papineau-Couture, Somers, and
      Weinzweig. (Har, 1955, 33 pp.) Some Fngr, MM &
      Ped. Biog. 8, some 3, 4, 5, 6 & 7.

8.2   DESCAVES, LUCETTE, ed. Les Nouveaux Contempo-
      rains, Premier Recueil.
      Pieces in The New Contemporaries, First collection,
      are attractive and most are easily accessible. Idio-
      matic writing for the piano. Progressive in difficulty.
      Admirable editing. Six works are contemporary
      enough to be included. (See 5.79, 5.126, 6.36, 8.6,
      8.58, and 8.86.) Titles in French. Contains music
      by Alain, Aubin, Bitsch, Chailley, Dutilleux, Lesur,
      Noël-Gallon, Revel, Roizenblat, Sauguet, Thiriet, and
      Tomasi. (Chou, 1965, 43 pp.) 12 pieces, 12 com-
      posers. Fngr, MM & Ped. 8, some 5 & 6.

8.3   Styles in 20th Century Piano Music.
      Splendid collection. Revised and extended since first
      published in 1951. Ten of the twelve works first pub-
      lished since 1950 are reviewed; others too difficult for
      this study. (See 5.153, 6.117, 6.149, 7.48, 7.94,
      8.38, 8.39, 8.70, and 8.82.) "Composers from 14 coun-
      tries are represented." Comments in German and
      English. Much music printed on each page. Contains
      music by Apostel, Bartók, Bennett, Blacher, Boulez,
      Burkhard, Casella, von Einem, Haba, Haubenstock-
      Ramati, Hauer, Jelinek, Kodály, Krenek, Martin, Mil-
      haud, Paccagnini, Petyrek, Poot, Pousseur, Reger,
      Schoenberg, Skalkottas, Stockhausen, Strauss, Szyman-
      owski, Tcherepnin, Wagner-Régeny, Webern, Wellesz,
      and Wladigeroff. (UE 12050E, 1968, 89 pp.) 35

pieces, 31 composers. Some MM & Ped.   Anal.
Biog.   8, some 6, 6 & 7.

GLOSSARY

(Terms not in Harvard Brief Dictionary of Music)

ARTICULATION. Refers, in a narrow sense, to staccato and/or legato manner of performance; more inclusively, nearly synonymous with phrasing.

COUNTER-MELODY. An independent melody, but secondary to the most important melody.

COUPLED WRITING. Melody doubled by second hand, usually at the octave. Coupled two-part writing has double notes in one hand duplicated by the other hand.

DOUBLE INFLECTION. A tone and its chromatic alteration sound together, or in immediate succession in different voices. Same as cross relation.

DOUBLE NOTES. Two different simultaneous notes in one hand.

EXTENDED INTERVALS, or EXTENSIONS. Wide-spaced intervals, where stretching between adjacent fingers is needed.

FIVE-FINGER POSITION. Narrowly, each finger is on consecutive diatonic tones; more broadly, no thumb-under is used.

GESTURE. A particularly striking rhythmic or melodic contour.

KEY SIGNATURE OMITTED. Indicates that, while music is tonal, keys change so frequently or so many accidentals are used that printing is more easily read when notes are natural unless otherwise indicated.

MELODY/ACCOMPANIMENT TEXTURE. Homophonic texture; that is, melody is supported by chords.

METERS, VARIABLE. Changing meters, such as 2/8 to 3/8 to 4/8 to 5/8. Meter signatures may be omitted.

MIRROR WRITING. One line moves opposite or contrary to another; c up to e would be reflected by c down to a-flat.

MODAL INTERCHANGE. Tonal center remains, but modes are changed.

NON-TONAL. Some common triads or important repeated single tones are present, but no specific tonality can be determined.

OFFBEAT. Part of a measure other than the principally accented one; for example, second or fourth beat in a 4/4 measure, or between usual beats.

ONE-LINE MUSIC. Melody only, no accompaniment.

POLYHARMONY, or POLYTONALITY. Two (or more) identifiable harmonies, or tonalities, sounding at same time.

RAGA. A melody-type in Hindu music.

ROTARY MOTION. Forearm rotates from left to right, or the reverse.

SCALE, DOUBLE HARMONIC. Like the major mode, but with lowered second and sixth tones.

SCALE, HUNGARIAN MAJOR. Like the mixolydian mode, but with raised second and fourth tones.

SCALE, HUNGARIAN MINOR. Like the aeolian mode, but with raised fourth and seventh tones.

SCALE, LYDIAN MINOR. Like the lydian mode, but with lowered sixth and seventh tones.

SCALE, MAJOR LOCHRIAN. Like the major mode, but with lowered fifth, sixth and seventh tones.

SCALE, OVERTONE. Like the lydian mode, but with lowered seventh tone.

SCALE, SUPER LOCHRIAN.   Like the phrygian mode, but
    with lowered fourth and fifth tones.

SCALE, SYNTHETIC.   Any scale formation not frequently
    found.

SECUNDAL HARMONY.   Chords based on the interval of the
    second.

SEGMENT OF TWELVE-TONE SET.   Tones selected from
    the twelve-tone set and used as a unit of organiza-
    tion.

SET TRANSFORMATION.   Order of tones in a twelve-tone
    set is changed, such as from the original order to
    its inversion, or to retrograde, or to retrograde in-
    version.

SHORT-LONG RHYTHM.   Rhythmic unit such as an eighth
    note followed by a quarter note; less common than the
    reverse.

STACCATO, FINGER.   Finger moves as a unit from the
    hand-knuckle for staccato touch.

STACCATO, FOREARM.   Hand and fingers move as a unit
    from the elbow joint for staccato touch.

STACCATO, HAND.   Hand and fingers move as a unit from
    the wrist joint for staccato touch.

TEXTURE, FULL.   Sound has many tones, often in a wide
    range.   Opposed to thin texture, where few tones
    are used.

TONALITY, REMOTE.   Tonal, but vague; perhaps a bass
    tone (tonic) is reiterated, but other tones are unre-
    lated.

TRIADS, FREELY ASSOCIATED.   Succession of common
    triads without regard for tonality.

TWELVE-TONE SET.   Same as twelve-tone series or
    twelve-tone row.

UNMETERED.   Meter (or time) signature is omitted; note
    values usually present, but there are no patterns

of values.

VOICE. A single melodic line. Same as part.

INDEX TO MUSICAL AND PIANISTIC FEATURES

ACCESSIBLE (easily understood) 2.15, 20, 32, 36, 55; 3.14, 15, 19, 32, 36, 37, 50, 73, 76, 84, 91, 97; 4.33, 44, 53, 55, 56, 60, 74, 85, 88, 92, 100, 140, 143, 148, 149, 151, 165, 166, 169; 5.7, 22, 36, 44, 47, 50, 54, 57, 58, 89, 98, 130, 135, 142, 148.

ADDED-NOTE CHORDS 2.21; 3.45, 56, 68, 83, 86, 114; 4.16, 43, 46, 48, 59, 93, 94, 97, 119, 126, 161, 165, 168; 5.16, 47. 63, 73, 85, 92, 97, 98, 101, 109, 118, 126, 130, 141, 149.

ALTERNATING HANDS see HANDS, ALTERNATING

ANALYSIS INCLUDED 2.9, 11, 12, 13, 21, 22, 23, 36, 37; 3.1, 8, 19, 22, 30, 31, 32, 36, 40, 42, 58, 60, 72, 86, 89, 95, 101; 4.2, 19, 29, 32, 40, 41, 46, 49, 56, 58, 59, 65, 100, 101, 111, 121, 124, 141, 150, 151, 159, 160, 164, 165, 166; 5.8, 13, 34, 35, 36, 69, 73, 74, 86, 87, 99, 102, 105, 109, 111, 130, 133, 154, 156.

ARPEGGIOS 5.29, 112, 118, 123, 160.

ARTICULATION VARIETY 2.5, 17, 20, 51; 3.8, 11, 22, 33, 59, 64, 110; 4.16, 24, 39, 44, 46, 49, 78, 79, 97, 111, 142, 144, 154, 168; 5.7, 10, 14, 23, 24, 34, 42, 46, 47, 53, 58, 78, 86, 107, 115, 118, 135, 149.

ATONAL 4.121; 5.155.

BIOGRAPHY INCLUDED 2.1, 3, 12; 3.3, 4, 5; 4.1, 3, 5, 6, 7, 10, 35, 46, 47, 66, 71, 75, 81, 96, 103, 104, 115, 116, 123, 144, 155; 5.2, 24, 49, 55, 75, 81, 82, 90, 91, 92, 96, 101, 144, 146, 150.

BROKEN DOUBLE NOTES OR CHORDS 1.5; 2.5, 21, 24, 27, 29, 30, 31, 43; 3.12, 16, 17, 32, 40, 48, 51,

73, 74, 79, 83, 84, 91, 106, 109, 114; 4.13, 18,
36, 44, 55, 56, 61, 62, 64, 68, 69, 75, 80, 85,
88, 90, 96, 98, 123, 126, 133, 140, 155, 156, 163,
166; 5.6, 10, 12, 15, 25, 32, 38, 43, 51, 52, 70,
95, 97, 98, 101, 116, 121, 124, 139, 147, 151, 152,
155, 156.

CANON 1.5; 2.15, 46, 48; 3.8, 45, 46, 84; 4.52, 112,
153;   5.7, 10, 118, 128, 147.

CHILDREN'S PIECES (especially) 1.3; 2.1, 3, 7, 13, 15,
17, 18, 19, 21, 22, 23, 26, 29, 32, 36, 37, 38, 40,
41, 43, 44, 49, 53, 55; 3.7, 9, 10, 15, 16, 17, 18,
20, 30, 32, 35, 36, 37, 43, 44, 45, 46, 55, 56, 57,
62, 63, 67, 71, 73, 75, 77, 78, 80, 81, 83, 84, 85,
102, 105, 107, 109, 110, 112, 113; 4.13, 24, 26,
39, 44, 53, 60, 76, 85, 89, 92, 97, 98, 105, 112,
113, 128, 133, 135, 136, 161; 5.29, 38, 48, 76,
91, 92, 95, 104, 112, 113, 118, 130, 143.

CHORDS, ADDED-NOTE   see   ADDED-NOTE CHORDS

CHORDS, ARPEGGIATED   see   ARPEGGIATED CHORDS

CHORDS, CLUSTER   see   CLUSTER CHORDS

CHORDS FREELY ASSOCIATED (no central tonality)   2.30,
42; 3.73; 4.14, 116; 5.108.

CHORDS, HARMONIC (block) 2.35; 3.81, 113, 114; 4.98,
128, 132, 135, 145, 163; 5.7, 10, 15, 24, 26, 27,
33, 76, 92, 93, 101, 103, 107, 110, 118, 125, 129,
132, 137, 143, 144, 147, 150, 160.

CHORDS, RAPID REPEATED   see   REPEATED CHORDS,
RAPID

CLUSTER CHORDS 2.9, 12; 3.77; 4.32, 68, 70, 71,
133, 135, 145, 159; 5.10, 127, 130, 156.

CONSERVATIVE 1.6; 2.6, 7, 13, 15, 29, 39, 51, 55;
3.13, 20, 32, 34, 35, 38, 46, 48, 55, 61, 63, 66,
89, 90, 106, 114; 4.10, 31, 34, 42, 44, 50, 56,
57, 65, 75, 78, 86, 103, 108, 125, 126, 129, 130,
131, 132, 137, 144, 146, 155, 156; 5.19, 22, 47,
57, 68, 75, 91, 96, 104, 112, 126, 145.

INDEX TO COMPOSERS AND COMPOSITIONS

ORDERING INSTRUCTIONS

Music described in this Guide may be had from your local music dealer or from the following central sources:

Joseph Boonin, Inc.
P. O. Box 2124
So. Hackensack, N. J.   07606
Tel. (201) 488-1450

de Keyser Music
6679 Hollywood Blvd.
Hollywood, Calif.   90028
Tel. (213) 465-5035

When ordering from either of the above two dealers, music may be described by the given index number only (1.1).   Be sure to specify quantities greater than one, and the desired shipping method.   Ways of shipping, from slowest, most economical to fastest, most expensive are: Special Fourth Class Rate (Book Rate); Special Handling; Special Delivery; Air Mail; and Air Mail Special Delivery.   Orders which do not specify preferred method will be sent Special Fourth Class Rate.

Orders totalling less than $25.00 will be shipped prepaid and billed on open account.   Those amounting to more than $25.00 will be answered by return mail with an itemized invoice, and the music will be shipped immediately upon receipt of remittance of the total.

Prices for individual items will be given on request. Include self-addressed stamped envelope.

Allow three weeks delivery time for music published in the U. S. A. or Canada; music published overseas may in many cases require rather more time.   Any item requiring more than ninety days to supply will be subject to a report contingent on publisher's information.   Items undergoing a permanent change in availability will be reported on receipt of order.   Music sent on definite order is not returnable unless defective in manufacture or incorrectly filled on order.

PUBLISHER INFORMATION

Abbreviation	Publisher	U. S. Agent
AE	Amberson Enterprises	GS
Al	G. Alsbach & Co.	Pet
AME	American Music Edition	Joseph Boonin, Inc.
AMP	Associated Music Publishers, Inc.	
A&S	Ahn & Simrock	Sal
Aug	Augener, Ltd.	Galx
Bär	Bärenreiter-Verlag	
Barry	Barry & Cia	B&H
B&B	Bote & Bock	AMP
Beek	Beekman Music, Inc.	Pr
Bel-M	Belwin-Mills	
B&H	Boosey & Hawkes, Inc.	
Bil	Editions Billaudot	Pr
BMI	Berandol Music, Ltd.	AMP
Bong	Edizioni Bongiovanni	Bel-M
Br&H	Breitkopf & Härtel	AMP
BrB	Broude Bros Music	
B&VP	Broekmans & Van Poppel	Pet
CBDM	Belgian Centre of Music Documentation	HE
CF	Carl Fischer, Inc.	
Chap	Chappell & Company, Inc.	
Chap-L	Chappell & Company, Ltd., London	Chap
Ches	J. & W. Chester, Ltd.	

Abbreviation	Publisher	U. S. Agent
Chou	Editions Choudens (see Bil)	
Cos	Editions Costallat (see Bil)	
Der	Derry Music Company	Sha
Dit	Oliver Ditson Company	Pr
Dob	Ludwig Doblinger Musikverlag	AMP
Don	Stitching Donemus	Pet
Du	Duchess Music Corporation	MCA
Dur	Durand & Cie	EV
Elk	Elkin & Company, Ltd.	Galx
EMB	Editio Musica Budapesta	B&H
EMM	Ediciones Mexicanas de Musica, A.C.	SMP
EMT	Editions Musicales Transatlantiques	Pr
Esc	Editions Max Eschig	AMP
EV	Elkan-Vogel Company	Pr
Faz	Musik Fazer	
FC	Franco Colombo	Bel-M
Fox	Sam Fox Publishing Company	
G&C	G&C Music Corporation	Chap
Gal	Galliard, Ltd.	Galx
Galx	Galaxy Music Corporation	
Geh	Carl Gehrmans Musikförlag	
Gen	General Music Publishing Company, Inc.	Frank Distributing Company
	Musikverlage Hans Gerig (see HG)	
GS	G. Schirmer, Inc.	
GVT	Gordon V. Thompson, Limited	
	Hansen, Wilhelm, Musik-forlag (see WH)	
Har	The Frederick Harris Music Co., Ltd.	
HE	Henri Elkan Music Publisher	
Hein	Heinrichshofen's Verlag	Pet

Abbreviation	Publisher	U. S. Agent
Hel	Helios Music Edition	Mark Foster
Heu	Heugel & Cie	Pr
HG	Musikverlage Hans Gerig	MCA
HiP	Highgate Press	Galx
Hin	Hinrichsen Edition, Ltd.	Pet
HL	Henry Lemoine & Cie	
HP	Henmar Press	Pet
IMI	Israel Music Institute	B&H
IMP	Israel Music Publications	MCA
IVi	Irmaos Vitale S/A	Lawrence J. Green 200 W. 57th St. N.Y. 10019
JF	J. Fischer & Bro.	Bel-M
Jos	Joshua Corporation	Gen
JW	Josef Weinberger	Pr
Led	Alphonse Leduc & Cie	
Leeds-NY	Leeds Music Corporation	MCA
Leeds-C	Leeds Music (Canada) Limited	MCA
	Henry Lemoine & Cie (see HL)	
Lit/Pet	Henry Litolff's Verlag	Pet
LR	Lee Roberts Music Publications	
Ly	Harald Lyche & Co's Musikförlag	Pet
MCA	MCA Music	
McK	Peter McKee Music Co.	Wat
Mer	Merion Music, Inc.	Pr
Merc	Mercury Music Corporation	Pr
Metr	Editions Metropolis	HE
Mil-L	Mills Music, London	Bel-M
Mil-NY	Mills Music, Inc.	
MJQ	MJQ	
M&M	McGinnis & Marx	

Abbreviation	Publisher	U.S. Agent
Mrk	Edward B. Marks Music Corporation	
Muz	Muzyka	MCA
Noël	Pierre Noël Editeur (See Bil)	
Noet	Otto Heinrich Noetzel Verlag	Pet
Nord	AB Nordiska Musikförlaget	
Norsk	Norsk Musikforlag A/S	
Nov	Novello & Company Ltd.	Bel-M
NVMP	New Valley Music Press of Smith College	
Ongaku	Ongaku-No-Tomo Sha Corporation	
Orc	Orchesis Publications	
Oxf	Oxford University Press	
Pan	Panton	B&H
PAU	Pan American Union	SMP
Peer	Peer International Corporation	SMP
Pet	C.F. Peters Corporation	
Pr	Theodore Presser Company	
PWM	Polskie Wydawnictwo Muzyczne	Mrk
Ric	G. Ricordi & Co., Milan	Bel-M
Ric-Ba	Ricordi Americana, Buenois Aires	Bel-M
Ric-Br	Ricordi Brasileira, Sao Paulo	Bel-M
Ric-L	G. Ricordi, London	Bel-M
Ron	Rongwen Music, Inc.	BrB
Row	R.D. Row Music Co., Inc.	CF
Sal	Editions Salabert	
SB	Summy-Burchard Company	
Scho	Schott & Co., Ltd.	Bel-M
ScS	B. Schott's Söhne	Bel-M
SF	Schott Frères	Pet
Sha	Shawnee Press, Inc.	
Shv	Statne hudobne vydavelstve (See Sup)	

Abbreviation	Publisher	U. S. Agent
Sim	N. Simrock	AMP
SMP	Southern Music Publishing Company, Inc.	
Sov	Soviet Composers	
St&B	Stainer & Bell Ltd.	Galx
Sup	Editio Supraphon	B&H
Tem	Alec Templeton	Sha
UE	Universal Edition	Pr
UWP	University of Washington Press	Galx
UME	Union Musical Española	AMP
VMP	Valley Music Press of Smith College	
Wat	Waterloo Music Company Limited	
	Joseph Weinberger (see JW)	
Weint	Weintraub Music Company	
WH	Wilhelm Hansen, Musik-forlag	GS
Zen	Edition Zen-On	
Zer	Edizioni Suvini Zerboni	MCA

Addenda

ICL	Israel Composers League	Mil-NY
Ton	P. J. Tonger Musikverlag	Pet